CYRANO deBERGERAC

Edmond Rostand

Prestwick House
LITERARY TOUCHSTONE CLASSICS™

P.O. Box 658 Clayton, Delaware 19938 • www.prestwickhouse.com

SENIOR EDITOR: Paul Moliken

EDITORS: Lisa M. Miller and Stacey MacPherson

COVER DESIGN: Kyle Price

PRODUCTION: Jerry Clark

Prestwick House
LITERARY TOUCHSTONE CLASSICS™

P.O. BOX 658 • CLAYTON, DELAWARE 19938
TEL: 1.800.932.4593
FAX: 1.888.718.9333
WEB: www.prestwickhouse.com

Prestwick House Teaching Units™, Activity Packs™, and Response Journals™ are the perfect complement for these editions. To purchase teaching resources for this book, visit www.prestwickhouse.com.

This Prestwick House edition is an unabridged republication of undated manuscripts with slight emendations of *Cyrano de Bergerac*.

ISBN: 978-1-58049-340-6

CYRANO de BERGERAC

By Edmond Rostand

CONTENTS

What are literary classics and why are they important?

A literary classic is a work of the highest excellence that says something important about life and the human condition—and says it with great artistry. It has withstood the test of time and is not bound by any specific time, place, or culture. For this reason, a classic is considered to have universal appeal and significance. It speaks to us today as forcefully as it spoke to readers when it was first written, and its power will continue to give future generations new perspectives on life.

Edmond Rostand was born on April 1, 1868, into a wealthy, refined French family. The young boy was encouraged to explore his imagination, and he had a book of his poems published in a literary magazine by the time he turned sixteen. Rostand went to college to become a lawyer, but a literary career interested him much more, and he never practiced law.

In 1890, Rostand married the poet Rosemonde Gérard, and they had two children.

After two unsuccessful attempts at writing dramas, his play *Les Romanesques* (*The Romancers*), written in 1894, became popular with the French public, and Rostand was finally a well-known author.

A famous French actor, Benoît-Constant Coquelin, persuaded Rostand to write a play that would showcase his wide range of acting abilities. Out of this association came the masterpiece for which Rostand is remembered, *Cyrano de Bergerac*. The story is loosely based on the life of Hercule Savinien Cyrano de Bergerac, who was not a great swordsman, but who did have a large nose—although not as large as Rostand's Cyrano—and was quite vain about it. *Cyrano de Bergerac,* however, marks the end of French dramatic Romanticism, which was soon overtaken by more naturalistic styles.

In 1901, strictly on the popularity of *Cyrano de Bergerac,* Rostand was elected to the Académie Française (French Academy), the prestigious French language institution. Rostand wrote only a few additional plays, none of which were well received. Despondent and ill, he retired to his estate in the country.

Rostand died on Dec. 2, 1918, a victim of the worldwide influenza pandemic.

Reading Pointers for Sharper Insights

1. To better appreciate *Cyrano de Bergerac*, consider some of the following themes that the play deals with:

   - Intelligence and inner worth are more valuable than physical beauty.
   - People tend to magnify their own faults or flaws, which can lead to low self-esteem and/or self-destructive behavior.
   - Deception often causes unfavorable consequences for both the deceiver and the deceived.
   - Honor, virtue, and moral purity are heroic qualities that are often intertwined with suffering and self-sacrifice.

2. It is important to consider some historical context with regard to two particular time periods: the time and place in which the action of the play occurs and the time and place in which Edmond Rostand wrote the play.

   A. The play is set in France between the years of 1640 and 1655.

      - France is involved in the Thirty Years' War, a war fought against the Holy Roman Empire mainly over trade routes.
      - France reaches its height in the areas of art, literature, and philosophy, which sets the standard for the rest of Europe.
      - Cardinal Richelieu has recently founded the French Academy, a society of intellectuals and writers.
      - Literature and poetry are discussed at intellectual gatherings called salons, which were popular among educated, aristocratic women and usually took place in the homes of such women.

B. Edmond Rostand wrote *Cyrano de Bergerac* in Paris, France, in 1897.

- France experiences rapid industrial growth and further growth of its many colonies.
- English physicist Joseph John Thomson discovers the electron.
- *The Invisible Man* by H. G. Wells and *Dracula* by Bram Stoker are published.
- Realism and naturalism dominate the arts, but a neo-romanticist movement also begins, of which Rostand is a part.

3. As stated above, the late nineteenth century was dominated by realism in the arts. The realist tradition involved frank depictions of everyday life and its mundane activities, important social or political themes, and depictions of the daily struggles people faced, especially those in the lower classes. Rostand, however, along with other artists of his time, broke out of this realist mode and looked back to the genre of Romanticism, a literary movement popular in Europe during the late 18th century. Romanticism involves the following characteristics:

- the depiction of intense emotion and expression
- the importance of action, movement, and drama
- a focus on the individual and his or her rebellion against social conventions

4. Be aware of numerous references by Rostand to other famous literary works and plays. For example, the balcony scene in *Cyrano de Bergerac* is a parody of the balcony scene in Shakespeare's *Romeo and Juliet*. Pay special attention, however, to the many references to Alexandre Dumas's 1844 novel *The Three Musketeers*. Rostand was a fan of Dumas's novel, and he both parodies and pays tribute to it in *Cyrano de Bergerac*.

5. Understand some of the symbols that occur in *Cyrano de Bergerac*:

- Cyrano's nose symbolizes several things. On the one hand, it symbolizes his best qualities: loyalty, virtue, bravery, and independence. It also symbolizes his character's biggest weakness: his insecurities when it comes to love.
- Cyrano's tears and Christian's blood on the last letter to Roxane symbolize the fact that the two men together made up one romantic hero.
- The white plume is a symbol of honor, bravery, purity, and moral integrity.

6. Understand some of the motifs that occur in the play:

- fighting and war
- poetry and letters
- the moon and the night sky
- society and its hierarchies
- Greek mythology and ancient heroes

I wished to dedicate this play to Cyrano's soul,
But since his soul has now passed into you,
Coquelin,[†] *it is to you that I dedicate it.*
                                    E.R.

†Terms marked in the text with (†) can be looked up in the Glossary for additional information.

9

Dramatis Personae

CYRANO DE BERGERAC[†]

CHRISTIAN DE NEUVILLETTE

COUNT DE GUICHE

RAGUENEAU

LE BRET

CARBON DE CASTEL-JALOUX

THE CADETS

LIGNIERE

DE VALVERT

A MARQUIS

SECOND MARQUIS

THIRD MARQUIS

MONTFLEURY

BELLEROSE

JODELET

CUIGY

BRISSAILLE

THE DOORKEEPER

A LACKEY

SECOND LACKEY

A BORE

A MUSKETEER

SECOND MUSKETEER

A SPANISH OFFICER

A PORTER

A BURGHER

HIS SON

A PICKPOCKET

A SPECTATOR

A GUARDSMAN

BERTRANDOU THE FIFER

A MONK

TWO MUSICIANS

THE POETS

THE PASTRY COOKS

ROXANE

SISTER MARTHA

LISE

THE BUFFET-GIRL

MOTHER MARGUERITE

THE DUENNA

SISTER CLAIRE

AN ACTRESS

THE PAGES

THE SHOP-GIRL

The CROWD, TROOPERS, BURGHERS, MARQUISES, MUSKETEERS, PICKPOCKETS, PASTRY COOKS, POETS, CADETS, COMEDIANS, ACTORS, VIOLINISTS, PAGES, CHILDREN, SPANISH SOLDIERS, SPECTATORS, INTELLECTUALS, NUNS, etc.

The first four acts take place in 1640; the fifth act takes place in 1655.

ACT I

A Performance at the Hotel de Bourgogne†

The hall of the Hotel de Bourgogne, in 1640. It is a sort of tennis court arranged and decorated for a theatrical performance.

The hall is oblong and seen from an angle, so that one of its sides forms the back of the right foreground, and meeting the left background, makes an angle with the stage, which is partly visible.

On both sides of the stage are benches. The curtain is made up of two tapestries which can be drawn aside. Above the proscenium are the royal arms. There are broad steps from the stage to the hall. On either side of these steps are the places for the violinists. The footlights consist of a row of candles.

There are two rows, one over the other, of side galleries. The highest row is divided into boxes. There are no seats in the pit of the hall, which is the real stage of the theater. At the back of the pit, some benches form steps, and underneath the steps is a staircase which leads to the upper seats. There is an improvised buffet containing candles, vases, glasses, plates of tarts, cakes, bottles, etc.

The entrance to the theater is in the center of the background, under the gallery of the boxes. A large door is half-open to let in the spectators. On the panels of this door, in different corners, and over the buffet, are red placards bearing the words, "La Clorise."

At the rising of the curtain, the hall is in semi-darkness, and still empty. The candle-holders are lowered in the middle of the pit, ready to be lighted.

Scene i

The public, arriving by degrees. TROOPERS, BURGHERS, LACKEYS, PAGES, *a* PICK-POCKET, *the* DOORKEEPER, *etc., followed by the* MARQUISES. CUIGY, BRISSAILLE, *the* BUFFET-GIRL, *the* VIOLINISTS, *etc.*

[*A confusion of loud voices is heard outside the door. A* TROOPER *enters hastily.*]

DOORKEEPER: [*going after him*] Wait! You must pay your fifteen sols!†
TROOPER: I get in free!
DOORKEEPER: How so?
TROOPER: I'm a soldier in the King's Cavalry!†
DOORKEEPER: [*to* SECOND TROOPER *who also enters*] And you?
SECOND TROOPER: I get in free as well. I'm a musketeer!
FIRST TROOPER: [*to the second*]
   The play doesn't begin until two. Let's have a bout with the foils to pass
   the time.

[*They begin fencing.*]

A LACKEY: [*entering*] Psst—Flanquin!
SECOND LACKEY: Is that you, Champagne?
FIRST LACKEY: [*taking cards and some dice out of his jacket pocket*]
   Look what I've brought. Let's play!
SECOND LACKEY: Good idea, my rogue friend!

[*They both sit down on the floor.*]

FIRST LACKEY: [*taking a candle-end from his pocket and lighting it*]
   I've stolen for us a little light from my master.
A GUARDSMAN: [*to a* SHOP-GIRL *who comes toward him*] How nice of you to
   come before the lights are lit!

[*He grabs her at the waist.*]

ONE OF THE FENCERS: [*receiving a thrust*] A hit!
ONE OF THE CARD-PLAYERS: A club!
GUARDSMAN: [*following the girl*] A kiss!
SHOP-GIRL: [*trying to free herself from his grasp*] Stop! They'll see us!
GUARDSMAN: [*drawing her to a dark corner*] Now they can't!
A MAN: [*sitting on the floor with some others who are all eating food*] By
   coming early, one can eat in comfort.

A **Burgher:** [*leading his* SON] Let's sit here, my son.

A **Card-Player:** Triple ace!

A **Man:** [*taking a bottle out from his jacket and seating himself on the floor*]
A drunkard should drink his Burgundy†...[*he drinks*] in the Hotel Burgundy!

Burgher: [*to his* SON] My God! One would think we've stumbled into some place of ill-repute! What with drunkards! [*He points with his cane to the drunk.*] Brawlers! [*One of the* FENCERS *jostles him.*] And gamblers! [*He stumbles into the midst of the* CARD-PLAYERS.]

Guardsman: [*behind the* BURGHER, *still teasing the* SHOP-GIRL] Come on, just one kiss!

Burgher: [*hurriedly pulling* HIS SON *away*] Good heavens! And to think that Rotrou† was played here!

His Son: Yes, and Corneille† too!

A **Troop of Pages:** [*entering hand-in-hand, dancing and singing*] Tra-la-la-la-la-la-la-la-la...

Doorkeeper: [*sternly, to the* PAGES]
You pages better behave yourselves. No pranks tonight!

First Page: [*with an air of wounded dignity*] Oh, sir! How can you even suspect that we would do such things? [*quickly, to the* SECOND PAGE, *the moment the* DOORKEEPER'S *back is turned*] Did you bring the string?

Second Page: Oh, yes—and a fish-hook with it!

First Page: Great! We'll fish for wigs from up in the gallery!

A **Pickpocket:** [*gathering about him some evil-looking youths*] Listen here, you young thieves. I'm about to give you your first lesson in stealing.

Second Page: [*calling up to other* PAGES *in the top galleries*] Have you all brought your peashooters?

Third Page: [*from above*] Oh yes, and peas too!

[*He blows peas down at the crowd.*]

Burgher's Son: [*to his father*] What's the name of the play tonight?

Burgher: *La Clorise.*

Son: Who wrote it?

Burgher: Balthazar Baro.† It's a play about...

[*He takes his* SON *by the arm and leads him away.*]

Pickpocket: [*to his students*] Look for lace knee-ruffles and cut them off!

A **Spectator:** [*to another, pointing to a corner of the gallery*] I was sitting up there, the first night of the 'Cid.'†

Pickpocket: [*making a gesture as of picking a pocket*] And with watches...

BURGHER: [*coming down again with his* SON] Soon you will see some great actors.

PICKPOCKET: [*making the type of gesture one would use when pulling something in a sneaky way, with little jerks of the hand*] And for handkerchiefs…

BURGHER: Montfleury†…

A VOICE FROM THE GALLERY: Light the lights!

BURGHER: Bellerose, L'Epy, La Beaupre, Jodelet!†

A PAGE: Here comes the buffet-girl!

BUFFET-GIRL: [*taking her place behind the buffet*] Oranges, milk, raspberry-water, cider…

[*A hubbub outside the door is heard.*]

A FALSETTO VOICE: Make way, you brutes!

A LACKEY: [*astonished*] The Marquises! Down here on the floor with us?

ANOTHER LACKEY: Oh, only for a moment, I'm sure.

[*Enter a band of young* MARQUISES.]

A MARQUIS: [*seeing that the hall is half empty*] What's this? We've arrived like common tradesmen—without disturbing anyone or stepping on their toes? For shame! [*recognizing some other gentlemen who have entered a little before him*] Cuigy! Brissaille!

[*They greet and embrace one another.*]

CUIGY: True to our word! We're here before the candles are lit.

MARQUIS: Enough! I'm so annoyed!

ANOTHER MARQUIS: Don't worry, Marquis, they're coming to light the candles now!

ENTIRE AUDIENCE: [*welcoming the entrance of the candle lighter*] Ah!

[*They form in groups around the candle-holders as they are lit. Some people have taken their seats in the galleries.* LIGNIERE, *disheveled but distinguished-looking, with disordered shirt-front is arm-in-arm with* CHRISTIAN DE NEUVILLETTE. CHRISTIAN, *who is dressed elegantly but a little out of fashion, seems preoccupied, and keeps looking at the boxes.*]

Scene ii

The same, with CHRISTIAN, LIGNIERE, *then* RAGUENEAU *and* LE BRET.

CUIGY: Ligniere!

BRISSAILLE: [*laughing*] Not drunk yet?

LIGNIERE: [*aside to* CHRISTIAN] Shall I introduce you? [CHRISTIAN *nods in assent.*] Baron de Neuvillette.

[*They exchange bows.*]

AUDIENCE: [*applauding as the first candelabra is lighted and drawn up*] Ah!

CUIGY: [*to* BRISSAILLE, *looking at* CHRISTIAN] Handsome fellow!

FIRST MARQUIS: [*who has overheard*] Pooh!

LIGNIERE: [*introducing them to* CHRISTIAN] Messieurs de Cuigy, de Brissaille.

CHRISTIAN: [*bowing*] Delighted to meet you.

FIRST MARQUIS: [*to the* SECOND] He's good-looking, but his fashion is a little out of date.

LIGNIERE: [*to* CUIGY] Monsieur de Neuvillette comes from Touraine.†

CHRISTIAN: Yes, I've only been in Paris for three weeks. Tomorrow I join the Guards, in the Cadets.†

FIRST MARQUIS: [*watching the people who are coming into the boxes*] There's Madame Aubry, the Chief-Justice's wife.

BUFFET-GIRL: Oranges, milk…

VIOLINISTS: [*tuning up*] La…La…

CUIGY: [*to* CHRISTIAN, *pointing to the hall, which is filling fast*] It's really getting crowded.

CHRISTIAN: Yes, indeed.

FIRST MARQUIS: The whole great world is arriving!

[*They recognize and name the different elegantly dressed ladies who enter the boxes, bowing low to them. The ladies send smiles in answer.*]

SECOND MARQUIS: Madame de Guemenee.

CUIGY: Madame de Bois-Dauphin.

FIRST MARQUIS: Adored by us all!

BRISSAILLE: Madame de Chavigny.

SECOND MARQUIS: Who plays with our poor hearts!

LIGNIERE: Ah, there's Corneille. He must be back from Rouen!†

BURGHER'S SON: [*to his father*] Is the Academy† here?

BURGHER: Oh yes, I see several members. There's Boudu, Boissat, and Cureau de la Chambre, Porcheres, Colomby, Bourzeys, Bourdon, Arbaud. Names that will live forever! How wonderful!

First Marquis: Attention! Our lady intellectuals have arrived! There is Barthenoide, Urimedonte, Cassandace, Felixerie...

Second Marquis: Ah, their names are exquisite! Do you know them all, Marquis?

First Marquis: I do indeed, every one!

Ligniere: [drawing Christian aside] My friend, I came here tonight to help you, but the lady you seek is not here. I shall go now and return to my vice.

Christian: [persuasively] No, please stay! You are songwriter to the court and the city alike. You know everyone! You are the one who can tell me who she is—the lady for whom I'm dying of love!

First Violin: [striking his bow on the desk] Gentlemen violinists!

[He raises his bow.]

Buffet-Girl: Macaroons, lemon-drink...

[The violins begin to play.]

Christian: Oh! I'm afraid that she is coquettish and refined! I fear I'm not intelligent enough for her! How can I dare speak with her? I'm only a shy and honest soldier—not very good with words at all. She always sits right there, on the right. Her box is still empty!

Ligniere: [making as if to leave] I must go.

Christian: [detaining him] No, please stay.

Ligniere: I cannot stay. D'Assoucy is waiting for me at the tavern. I'll die of thirst here.

Buffet-Girl: [passing before him with a tray] Orange drink?

Ligniere: Ugh!

Buffet-Girl: Milk?

Ligniere: Pooh!

Buffet-Girl: Wine?

Ligniere: [to Christian] Oh, if you insist—I shall stay awhile longer. Now let me try a little of that wine.

[He sits by the buffet; the girl pours some out for him.]

Audience: [crying out joyously and excitedly as a plump little man enters] Ah! Ragueneau!

Ligniere: [to Christian] It's the famous tavern-keeper Ragueneau.

RAGUENEAU: [*dressed in the Sunday clothes of a pastry-cook, going up quickly to* LIGNIERE] Sir, have you seen Monsieur de Cyrano?

LIGNIERE: [*introducing him to* CHRISTIAN] The pastry-cook of the actors and the poets!

RAGUENEAU: [*overcome*] You praise me too highly!

LIGNIERE: Oh, stop! You are a great patron of the arts!

RAGUENEAU: Well, it is true that poets do come to my bakery...

LIGNIERE: To buy on credit! You yourself are a talented poet too.

RAGUENEAU: So they tell me.

LIGNIERE: You're mad about poetry!

RAGUENEAU: It is true that, for an ode...

LIGNIERE: You give a tart!

RAGUENEAU: Well, just a little tart.

LIGNIERE: Oh, you're being modest! Now, what do you give for a triolet?

RAGUENEAU: Oh, maybe a small roll or two.

LIGNIERE: [*severely*] Oh, come on! You give milk-rolls, the best kind! And as for the theater, which you love just as much as poetry...

RAGUENEAU: Oh, I adore the theater!

LIGNIERE: You pay with pastries! Now, tell me, how much did your ticket tonight cost you?

RAGUENEAU: Four custards and fifteen cream-puffs. [*He looks around on all sides.*] Monsieur Cyrano is not here? How strange.

LIGNIERE: Why?

RAGUENEAU: Montfleury is playing tonight!

LIGNIERE: Oh, yes, the fat fool is playing the role of Phedon tonight. But why should Cyrano care about it?

RAGUENEAU: Haven't you heard? He hates Montfleury and has forbidden him to show his face on stage for a whole month!

LIGNIERE: [*drinking his fourth glass of wine*] So?

RAGUENEAU: Montfleury will play! Unless...

CUIGY: [*who has joined them*] Cyrano can't stop him.

RAGUENEAU: That is what I've come to see!

FIRST MARQUIS: Who is this Cyrano?

CUIGY: A fellow who certainly knows how to handle a sword.

SECOND MARQUIS: Is he of noble birth?

CUIGY: Noble enough. He's a cadet in the Guards. [*He points to a gentleman who is going up and down the hall as if searching for someone.*] But his friend, Le Bret, over there, can tell you more about him. [*He calls him.*] Le Bret! [LE BRET *comes over to them.*] Are you looking for Cyrano?

LE BRET: Yes, and I'm beginning to worry.

CUIGY: He's an extraordinary man, isn't he?

LE BRET: [*tenderly*] He is the rarest, most delightful man on earth!

RAGUENEAU: A poet!

CUIGY: A soldier!

BRISSAILLE: A philosopher!

LE BRET: A musician!

LIGNIERE: And such a striking appearance!

RAGUENEAU: No painter today can do him justice! Only the wild and whimsical Jacques Callot,[†] if he were still alive, could have painted Cyrano's portrait. He'd have placed him in some fantastic setting and made Cyrano the maddest fighter there—with his triple-plumed hat and six-tailed jacket and his sword sticking up beneath his cloak like the proud tail of a rooster. He is a true swashbuckler—as bold as the fiercest soldier in Gascony![†] Above his collar he carries a nose—and my good lords, what a nose it is! When people see it, they immediately think it's a false nose. They think it's a joke and that soon Cyrano will take it off. But, alas, Cyrano never takes it off.

LE BRET: [throwing back his head] True, he keeps it on—and will maim any man who dares to remark on it!

RAGUENEAU: [proudly] His sword is one half the shears of Fate!

FIRST MARQUIS: [shrugging his shoulders] He won't come.

RAGUENEAU: I say he will come! And I'll wager you a chicken à la Ragueneau!

THE MARQUIS: [laughing] Agreed!

[Murmurs of admiration are heard in the hall. ROXANE has just appeared in her box. She seats herself in front, her DUENNA sits at the back. CHRISTIAN, who is paying the BUFFET-GIRL, does not see her entrance.]

SECOND MARQUIS: [with little cries of joy] Ah, gentlemen, she is exquisite—adorable—ravishing!

FIRST MARQUIS: She's as sweet as a peach smiling at a strawberry!

SECOND MARQUIS: And so fresh and cool! Any man approaching her might catch a chill at the heart!

CHRISTIAN: [Raising his head, he sees ROXANE and catches LIGNIERE by the arm.] It is she!

LIGNIERE: Ah! Is it she?

CHRISTIAN: Yes. Quickly, tell me her name! Oh, I am afraid.

LIGNIERE: [sipping his wine] Madeleine Robin—called Roxane. She's witty, charming, quite an intellectual.

CHRISTIAN: Woe is me!

LIGNIERE: Unmarried, an orphan, the cousin of Cyrano, whom we were just speaking about.

[*At this moment, an elegant nobleman, with blue ribbon across his breast, enters the box, and talks with* ROXANE, *standing.*]

CHRISTIAN: [*alarmed*] Who is that man?

LIGNIERE: [*who has become tipsy, winking at him*] That's Count de Guiche. He's in love with her, but he happens to be married to the niece of Armand de Richelieu.† Wants to set Roxane up with a certain sorry fellow by the name of Valvert—a viscount. Why Valvert? Because he's very accommodating, if you get my meaning! She won't agree to it, of course, but de Guiche is powerful, and can persecute a girl like her. I myself have actually composed a song in which I expose his nasty little plan. Oh, he must hate me! The end really hits home! Listen!

[*He gets up, staggering, and raises his glass, ready to sing.*]

CHRISTIAN: No. I'm leaving.

LIGNIERE: Where are you going?

CHRISTIAN: To find this Monsieur de Valvert!

LIGNIERE: Don't be so rash! He will kill you before you harm him. [*calling his attention to* ROXANE *with a look*] Stay right there—she's looking at you.

CHRISTIAN: It's true!

[*He stands looking at her. The group of* PICKPOCKETS *see him standing there in an open-mouthed daze. They draw near to him.*]

LIGNIERE: 'Tis I who am going. I am thirsty! And they are expecting me in the taverns!

[*He goes out, reeling.*]

LE BRET: [*who has been all around the hall, coming back to* RAGUENEAU *with a look of reassurance*] No sign of Cyrano.

RAGUENEAU: [*incredulously*] But still…

LE BRET: I'm hoping he hasn't seen the playbill.

AUDIENCE: Begin, begin!

Scene iii

The same, with all but LIGNIERE; DE GUICHE, VALVERT, *then* MONTFLEURY.

A MARQUIS: [*watching* DE GUICHE, *who comes down from* ROXANE'S *box and crosses the pit surrounded by obsequious noblemen, among them the* VISCOUNT DE VALVERT] He pays a fine court, your de Guiche!

SECOND MARQUIS: [*with distaste*] Another Gascon!

FIRST MARQUIS: Yes, but a cold and clever Gascon—that's the stuff success is made of! Believe me, we had best make our bow to him.

[*They go toward* DE GUICHE.]

SECOND MARQUIS: What fine ribbons, Count de Guiche! What would you call the color? 'Kiss me, my darling,' or 'Timid Fawn?'

DE GUICHE: I call it 'Sick Spaniard.'†

FIRST MARQUIS: Very appropriate! Thanks to your valor, things will soon go ill for Spain in Flanders.

DE GUICHE: I'm going up to sit on the stage. Won't you come along? [*He goes toward the stage, followed by the* MARQUISES *and gentlemen. Turning, he calls to de* VALVERT.] Come, Valvert!

CHRISTIAN: [*who is watching and listening, starts when he hears this name*] The Viscount! I'll throw my glove in his face! [*He puts his hand in his pocket and finds there the hand of a* PICKPOCKET *who is about to rob him. He turns around.*] What...?

PICKPOCKET: Oh!

CHRISTIAN: [*holding him tightly*] I was looking for my glove.

PICKPOCKET: [*smiling piteously*] And you found a hand instead. [*changing his tone and whispering quickly*] Let me go and I'll tell you a secret!

CHRISTIAN: [*still holding him*] What is it?

PICKPOCKET: Ligniere—your friend who just left...

CHRISTIAN: What about him?

PICKPOCKET: His life is in danger. He wrote a song which has offended some very powerful people. A hundred men—I am one of them—will be after him tonight.

CHRISTIAN: A hundred men! Who hired them?

PICKPOCKET: I cannot say. It's a secret—

CHRISTIAN: Oh!

PICKPOCKET: [*with great dignity*] Of the profession.

CHRISTIAN: Where are the men posted?

PICKPOCKET: At the Porte de Nesle. On his way home. Warn him.

CHRISTIAN: [*letting go of his wrists*] But where can I find him?

PICKPOCKET: Go around to all the taverns—The Golden Wine Press, The Pine Cone, The Bursting Belt, The Two Torches, The Three Funnels, and leave a word at each one that should put him on his guard.

CHRISTIAN: I'm on my way! Oh, the scoundrels! A hundred men against one!

[*looking lovingly at* ROXANE] Ah, to leave her! [*looking with rage at* DE VALVERT] And him! But save Ligniere I must!

[*He hurries out.* DE GUICHE, DE VALVERT, *and the* MARQUISES *have all disappeared behind the curtain to take their places on the benches placed on the stage. The pit is quite full; the galleries and boxes are also crowded.*]

AUDIENCE: Begin the play!

A BURGHER: [*whose wig is drawn up on the end of a string by a page in the upper gallery*] My wig!

CRIES OF DELIGHT: He's bald! Bravo, pages! Ha ha ha!

BURGHER: [*furious, shaking his fist*] Little villains!

LAUGHTER AND CRIES: [*beginning very loud, and dying gradually away*] Ha! ha! ha! ha! ha! ha!

[*There is total silence.*]

LE BRET: [*astonished*] Why the sudden silence? [*A* SPECTATOR *says something to him in a low voice*] Is it true?

THE SPECTATOR: I have just heard it on good authority.

MURMURS: [*spreading through the hall*] Shhh!—Is it him?—No!—Yes, I say!—In the box with the bars in front!—The Cardinal!—The Cardinal!—The Cardinal!

A PAGE: The devil! We'll have to behave ourselves now!

[*A knock is heard upon the stage. Everyone is motionless. There is a pause.*]

VOICE OF A MARQUIS: [*in the silence, behind the curtain*] Snuff that candle out!

ANOTHER MARQUIS: [*putting his head through the opening in the curtain*] A chair!

[*A chair is passed from hand to hand, over the heads of the spectators. The* MARQUIS *takes it and disappears, after blowing some kisses to the boxes.*]

A SPECTATOR: Silence!

[*Three knocks are heard on the stage. The curtains part. The* MARQUISES *in arrogant attitudes are seated on each side of the stage. The scene represents a pastoral landscape. Four little candelabra light the stage; the violins play softly.*]

LE BRET: [*in a low voice to* RAGUENEAU] Montfleury is about to come onstage?

RAGUENEAU: Yes, it is he who begins.

LE BRET: Cyrano isn't here.

RAGUENEAU: I suppose I've lost my wager then.

LE BRET: All for the better!

[*A note on the bagpipes is heard, and* MONTFLEURY *enters, enormously fat, in shepherd's dress, a hat wreathed with roses drooping over one ear, blowing into a ribboned bagpipe.*]

AUDIENCE: [*applauding*] Bravo, Montfleury! Montfleury!

MONTFLEURY: [*after bowing low, begins his part*]
    Happy is the man who dwells alone
    Far from the pomp of court and crowd
    In a solitary wood, where gentle breezes—

A VOICE: [*from the middle of the pit*] Scoundrel! Didn't I forbid you to show your face here for a month?

[*A general stupor ensues. Everyone turns around. The* CROWD *murmurs.*]

DIFFERENT VOICES: Hey?—What?—What's going on?

[*The people stand up in the boxes to look.*]

CUIGY: It's him!

LE BRET: [*terrified*] Cyrano!

THE VOICE: King of clowns! Leave the stage this instant!

AUDIENCE: [*indignantly*] Oh!

MONTFLEURY: But—

THE VOICE: Do you dare defy me?

DIFFERENT VOICES: [*from the pit and the boxes*] Shhh! Enough! Keep going, Monfleury—don't be afraid!

MONTFLEURY: [*in a trembling voice*] Happy is the man who dwells—

THE VOICE: [*more fiercely*]
    Prince of buffoons! Must I come and give you a taste of my cane?

[*A hand holding a cane starts up over the heads of the spectators.*]

MONTFLEURY: [*in a voice that trembles more and more*] Happy is the man—

[*The cane is shaken.*]

THE VOICE: Off the stage!

AUDIENCE: Oh!

MONTFLEURY: [*choking*] Happy is the man who—

CYRANO: [*appearing suddenly in the pit, standing on a chair, his arms crossed, his hat cocked fiercely, his mustache bristling, his nose terrible to see*] I shall be angry in a minute!

[*A sensation ripples throughout the theater.*]

Scene iv

The same, with CYRANO, *then* BELLEROSE *and* JODELET.

MONTFLEURY: [*to the* MARQUISES] Come to my help, my lords!

A MARQUIS: [*carelessly*] Oh, go on, Montfleury, keep acting.

CYRANO: If you do, I'll cuff your face, fat man!

MARQUIS: That's enough!

CYRANO: And you marquises! I advise all of you to hold your tongues, or else each one of you will get a taste of my cane!

ALL THE MARQUISES: [*rising*] That's enough! Montfleury—

CYRANO: If he doesn't get off the stage this minute, I'll cut off his ears and slit him up like a roasted pig!

A VOICE: But—

CYRANO: Out he goes!

ANOTHER VOICE: Yet—

CYRANO: Is he not gone yet? [*He makes the gesture of turning up his cuffs.*] Good! I shall mount the stage now and carve up this fine, fat Italian sausage!

MONTFLEURY: [*trying to be dignified*] You outrage Thalia† when you insult me!

CYRANO: [*very politely*] You, Sir, are not acquainted in the least with that muse! But if she ever had the questionable pleasure of meeting you, you fat dullard, she would be inspired to kick you in the backside!

AUDIENCE: Montfleury! Montfleury! Come, go on and play!

CYRANO: [*to those who are calling out*]
Have a care, all of you! If you keep on, you're liable to rouse my sword right out of its scabbard!

[*The circle around him widens.*]

THE CROWD: [*drawing back*] Stay back from him! Beware!

CYRANO: [to MONTFLEURY] Leave the stage! [*The* CROWD *begins to murmur and to come nearer to* CYRANO.] Did someone speak?

[*The* CROWD *draws back again.*]

A VOICE: [*singing at the back*]
>   Monsieur de Cyrano
>   Such a tyrant today
>   Oh, why won't he just go?
>   So that we can see the play!

AUDIENCE: [*singing*] *La Clorise! La Clorise!*

CYRANO: Let me hear you sing that foolish little song once more and I'll slaughter every man in this theater!

A BURGHER: Oh, do you think yourself Samson?

CYRANO: Yes, Samson! Will you lend me your jawbone,† Sir?

A LADY: [*in the boxes*] This is outrageous!

A LORD: Scandalous!

A BURGHER: Most annoying!

A PAGE: Hilarious!

AUDIENCE: [*hissing*] Montfleury! Cyrano!

CYRANO: Silence!

AUDIENCE: [*wildly excited*] Woof! Woof!—Quack! Quack!—Cock-a-doodle-doo!

CYRANO: I order you all to—

A PAGE: Meow!

CYRANO: I order silence! And I challenge every man here! Come, all you young heroes! I'll write down your names and give each of you a number—everyone will get their turn! Come now, who wants to be first? You, Sir? No? You? No? Come on, the first opponent will be done away with honorably and sent straight to glory! Come now, who wants to die? Hold up your hands! [*a silence*] What is it? Too modest to face my naked sword? No one? Not one name? Good, then I shall proceed. [*turning toward the stage, where* MONTFLEURY *waits in agony*] This theater must be cured of this boil! [*He puts his hand on his sword.*] And if it won't leave of its own accord, then I shall have to lance it!

MONTFLEURY: I—

CYRANO: [*leaves his chair, and settles himself in the middle of the circle which has formed*] I will clap my hands three times, you full moon! On the third clap, I want to see you eclipse yourself!

AUDIENCE: [*amused*] Ah!

CYRANO: [*clapping his hands*] One!

MONTFLEURY: I—

A Voice: [*in the boxes*] Stay!

Audience: [*divided*] Stay!—Go!—No, stay!

Montfleury: I think, gentlemen—

Cyrano: Two!

Montfleury: I think it would be wise if I—

Cyrano: Three!

[Montfleury *suddenly disappears. There is a tempest of laughs, whistles and catcalls.*]

Audience: Coward! Come back!

Cyrano: [*delighted, sits back in his chair, arms crossed*] Come back if you dare!

A Burgher: Call for the speaker of the theater!

[Bellerose *comes forward and bows.*]

The Boxes: Ah! Here's Bellerose!

Bellerose: [*elegantly*] My noble lords—

Audience: No! Give us Jodelet instead!

Jodelet: [*advancing, speaking in an exaggerated nasal voice*] Miserable calves!

Audience: [*laughing*] Bravo, go on!

Jodelet: No bravos, Sirs! The fat tragedian, whom you all love, has had to—

Audience: That coward!

Jodelet: —was obliged to go.

Audience: Call him back!

Some: No!

Others: Yes!

A Young Man: [*to* Cyrano] But, Sir, why do you hate Montfleury so much?

Cyrano: [*graciously, still seated*] Young man, I have two reasons—either will suffice. First, he is a terrible actor. He heaves up his lines as though they were buckets of water drawn clumsily from a well, when instead, they should soar from his lips like the lightest of birds. The second reason...well, that's my secret.

A Burgher: [*behind him*] Shame on you! You deprive us of *La Clorise*! I must insist—

Cyrano: [*turning his chair toward the* Burgher, *respectfully*] You old mule! The verses of Baro are worthless trash! You should thank me for stopping the play!

LADY INTELLECTUALS: [*in the boxes*] Our Baro! Oh dear! How dare he!

CYRANO: [*turning his chair toward the boxes gallantly*] Fair ladies! Bloom and radiate, fill us with longing, intoxicate us with your beauty, charm death with your sweet smiles, inspire poetry—but don't attempt to judge it!

BELLEROSE: We must give back the entrance fees!

CYRANO: [*turning his chair toward the stage*] Bellerose, that's the smartest thing anyone has said all afternoon! You know how I love the theater and its actors. Therefore, I would never intentionally rend a tear in Thespis'† sacred cloak! [*He rises and throws a bag onto the stage.*] Catch then the purse I throw and hold your peace!

AUDIENCE: [*dazzled*] Ah!—Oh!

JODELET: [*catching the bag skillfully and weighing it*] At this price, Sir, you are welcome to come and stop the play anytime!

AUDIENCE: Boo! Boo!

JODELET: Even if we all get booed!

BELLEROSE: Clear out the hall!

JODELET: Everybody out this minute!

[*The people begin to go out, while* CYRANO *looks on with satisfaction. But the* CROWD *soon stops on hearing the following scene, and everyone remains where they are. The women, who, with their cloaks on, are already standing up in the boxes, stop to listen, and finally reseat themselves.*]

LE BRET: [*to* CYRANO] You are mad!

A BORE: [*coming up to* CYRANO] The great actor Montfleury! How could you? Shame on you! Don't you know he's protected by the Duke of Candal! Do you have a patron?

CYRANO: No!

BORE: No patron?

CYRANO: None!

BORE: What! No great lord to shield you with his name?

CYRANO: [*irritated*] No, I've told you twice! Must I tell you again? I have no protector...[*He puts his hand on his sword.*] but I do have a protectress—right here!

BORE: But now you must leave town, then.

CYRANO: Well, that depends!

BORE: The Duke has a long arm, you know!

CYRANO: But not so long as mine, when it is lengthened out [*He shows his sword.*] ...with this!

BORE: But do you really dare...?

CYRANO: Oh, I certainly do!

BORE: But—

CYRANO: Get out now! Go!

BORE: But I—

CYRANO: Go! Or tell me why you stare at my nose!

THE BORE: [*petrified*] I—

CYRANO: [*walking straight up to him*] Well, what's so strange about it?

BORE: [*drawing back*] My lord, you're mistaken!

CYRANO: Is it soft and dangling, like an elephant's trunk?

BORE: [*still drawing back*] I never—

CYRANO: Is it crooked, like an owl's beak?

BORE: I—

CYRANO: Do you see a wart upon the tip?

BORE: No—

CYRANO: Is there a fly upon it? What is there to stare at?

BORE: Oh!

CYRANO: What do you see?

BORE: But I've been so careful not to look!

CYRANO: Oh? Why is that?

BORE: I was—

CYRANO: Oh! It disgusts you!

BORE: Sir!

CYRANO: Are you sickened by its color?

BORE: Please, Sir!

CYRANO: Or it's shape?

BORE: No, on the contrary!

CYRANO: Why then that look of distaste? Do you think it's too large, perhaps?

BORE: [*stammering*] No, it's small! Quite small! It's minute!

CYRANO: Minute! How dare you accuse me of having a small nose!

BORE: Heaven help me!

CYRANO: My nose is enormous, you snub-nosed, meddling idiot! And let it be said that I am proud to possess such an appendage! 'Tis well known that a large nose indicates an affable soul, one kind and courteous, liberal and brave, just like myself! Such qualities you could never hope to have, you hateful wretch! For that dull face which my hand will soon slap is as empty...[*He slaps him.*]

BORE: Ouch!

CYRANO: ...of pride, of glory, of feeling, of poetry and godlike spark—in fact, as empty as all that is embodied by my big nose, [*He turns him by the shoulders.*] as what my boot will soon meet! [*He kicks him in the backside.*]

BORE: [running away] Help! Call the Guard!

CYRANO: Here's a word of advice for any other fool who might find something amusing about the middle of my face. Let it be known that if the jester is a nobleman, he will not just taste my boot but will taste my steel instead!

DE GUICHE: [who, with the MARQUISES, has come down from the stage] He's becoming a nuisance!

DE VALVERT: [shrugging his shoulders] He's quite arrogant!

DE GUICHE: Won't anyone silence him?

DE VALVERT: I'll take the challenge. I'll treat him to one of my quips! See here! [With a conceited air, he goes up to CYRANO, who is watching him.] Sir, your nose is...hmm...it is...very big!

CYRANO: [gravely] Very!

DE VALVERT: [laughing] Ha!

CYRANO: [calmly] Is that all?

DE VALVERT: What do you mean?

CYRANO: Ah no, young man! That was a trifle short! You might have said at least a hundred things by varying the tone. Shall I give you a few examples?

Aggressive: "Sir, if I had such a nose, I'd amputate it!"

Friendly: "It must annoy you when it dips into your drink. You really should have a specially shaped goblet, I think!"

Descriptive: " 'Tis a rock, a peak, a cape, a peninsula!"

Curious: "What is the purpose of that large container? Do you keep your pens and ink in it?"

Gracious: "Oh, how you must love the birds! I see you've made them a nice perch for their tiny feet!"

Hostile: "When you enjoy your pipe and the smoke spouts from your nose, the neighbors must think the chimney's on fire!"

Considerate: "When you stroll, keep your head bowed low, else head over heels you just might go!"

Tender: "Oh, someone please get a small umbrella made, else in the sun its bright color might fade!"

Pedantic: "Only such a beast as Aristophanes' hippocampelephantocamelos[†] could have possessed such a large lump of flesh and bone beneath its forehead!"

Flippant: "What a fashionable hook to hang your hat on!"

Emphatic: "No wind but the Arctic blast would be strong enough to give you a cold, oh majestic nose!"

Dramatic: "When it bleeds, it's like the Red Sea!"

Admiring: "Oh, what a perfect sign for a perfume shop!"

Lyrical: "Is that a conch? And you, a Triton?"[†]

Simple: "Is that monument open for public viewing?"

Rustic: "Is that thing a nose? No, it must be a dwarf pumpkin, or a prize watermelon!"

Military: "Aim that cannon at the enemy and blast away!"

Practical: "Put it in the lottery! I'm sure it would be the biggest prize!"

Or, in a parody of Pyramus, "Behold the nose that mars the beauty of its owner's face. How red with shame it is, the traitor!"†

All of these things you might have said, if you were a man of wit and letters in the slightest. But, sadly, of wit you never had an atom, and of letters you have only three—and they spell Ass! And even if you were intelligent enough to think of witty remarks like the ones I just listed, you would not have been able to utter a single one of them. Because I allow such jokes only when spoken by myself, and never by any other man that breathes!

DE GUICHE: [*trying to draw away the dismayed* DE VALVERT] Come away, Viscount!

DE VALVERT: [*choking with rage*] Listen to this arrogant lout! A barbarian who wears no gloves…who comes out in public without any ribbons and lace!

CYRANO: True, all my elegances are within. I do not dress up like a pretentious dandy when I go out. But I'll tell you this: I groom myself more thoroughly than you. I would never venture out in public with a soiled conscience, a tarnished honor, or scruples grimy and dull. I do not adorn myself with gems and ribbons, like you. Instead, I decorate myself with truth, independence and a clean soul. I am not ornamented with tassels and lace but with proud and brave exploits instead. My spirit is sharper than your stiff mustache. When I walk among the crowds and chattering groups, I make Truth ring bravely out like a clash of spurs!

DE VALVERT: But, Sir—

CYRANO: I wear no gloves? And what of that? I had one, the remaining one of an old pair. And, not having any other use for it, I threw it in the face of some young fool.

DE VALVERT: Base scoundrel! Stupid lout!

CYRANO: [*taking off his hat, and bowing as if the* VISCOUNT *had introduced himself*] Oh, delighted to meet you! And I am Cyrano Savinien Hercule de Bergerac.

[*Laughter erupts throughout the* CROWD.]

DE VALVERT: [*angrily*] Buffoon!

CYRANO: [*crying out as if in pain*] Aie! Aie!

DE VALVERT: [*who was going away, turns back*] What on earth is the fellow saying now?

CYRANO: [*with grimaces of pain*] It must be moved—it's getting stiff! This is what happens when it's been unused for too long! Aie!

DE VALVERT: What is the matter with you?

CYRANO: The cramp! I have a cramp in my sword!

DE VALVERT: [*drawing his own sword*] So be it!

CYRANO: You shall feel a charming little stroke!

DE VALVERT: [*contemptuously*] Poet!

CYRANO: Yes, a poet, Sir! And to demonstrate my skills as such, I will compose a ballade as we fight.

DE VALVERT: A ballade?

CYRANO: Do you not know what a ballade is?

DE VALVERT: But—

CYRANO: [*reciting, as if repeating a lesson*] Know then that the ballade should contain three eight-versed couplets...

DE VALVERT: [*stamping his foot*] Oh!

CYRANO: [*still reciting*] And an envoi of four lines...

DE VALVERT: You—

CYRANO: I'll make one as we fight, and on the last line, I shall thrust my sword home.

DE VALVERT: No!

CYRANO: No? [*declaiming loudly*] Ballade of the duel between de Bergerac and a fool—here in the Hotel Burgundy!

DE VALVERT: What's all that?

CYRANO: That is the title.

AUDIENCE: [*greatly excited*] Quiet!—Make room!—Fair play!—What sport!

[*A circle of curious spectators forms in the pit. The* MARQUISES *and* OFFICERS *mingle with the common people. The* PAGES *climb on each other's shoulders to see better. All the* WOMEN *stand up in the boxes. To the right stand* DE GUICHE *and his retinue. To the left are* LE BRET, RAGUENEAU, CYRANO, *etc.*]

CYRANO: [*shutting his eyes for a second*] Wait while I choose my lines. Ah, now I have them!

[*He matches each action to each word.*]

> I lightly doff my hat down low,
> And, freeing hand and heel,
> My heavy cloak away I throw,
> And I draw my polished steel.
> Graceful as Phoebus,[†] round I wheel,
> With swiftness and skill alike,
> "Careful now," I say with zeal,
> For at the end of the refrain I shall strike!

[*They begin fencing.*]

> Better for you had you lain low.
> Where shall I hit you? In the heel?
> Or how about the heart, my worthless foe?
> Or in the hip, and make you kneel?
> Oh, for the music of clashing steel!
> Where shall I land my spike?
> 'Twill be in the belly the stroke I steal,
> When, at the end of the refrain I shall strike!
>
> Oh, for a word that rhymes with "o"!
> You wriggle, so white, my eel!
> Your face is as pale as fresh snow,
> As I parry the point of your steel.
> Oh there, a thrust you hoped I'd feel!
> But alas, you missed, little tyke!
> Now we're nearing the close of this deal.
> Watch out! At the end of the refrain I strike!

[*He declaims solemnly.*]

> Refrain:
> And now I shall make you kneel.
> Pray for your soul if you like!
> I thrust [*He thrusts.*] and your fate I seal,
> As at the end of the refrain—[DE VALVERT *staggers;* CYRANO *salutes.*]
> I strike![†]

[*Acclamations and applause rise from the boxes. Flowers and handkerchiefs are thrown down. The* OFFICERS *surround* CYRANO, *congratulating him.* RAGUENEAU *dances for joy.* LE BRET *is happy, but anxious.* DE VALVERT'S *friends hold him up and bear him away.*]

AUDIENCE: [*with one long shout*] Ah!

A TROOPER: 'Tis superb!

A WOMAN: A pretty stroke!

RAGUENEAU: A marvel!

LE BRET: Oh, madman!

AUDIENCE: [*presses around* CYRANO, *shouting*] Compliments!—Bravo!— Quite unsurpassed!

A WOMAN'S VOICE: There's a hero for you!

A MUSKETEER: [advancing to CYRANO with outstretched hand] Sir, permit me
    to say that you are a fine swordsman—and I am a good judge of such
    things. I stamped my feet to show my admiration!

[He goes away.]

CYRANO: [to CUIGY] Who is that gentleman?
CUIGY: Why, that's D'Artagnan!†
LE BRET: [to CYRANO, taking his arm] I need a word with you!
CYRANO: Wait—let the crowd go. [to BELLEROSE] May I stay?
BELLEROSE [respectfully] Of course!

[Cries are heard outside.]

JODELET: [who has looked out] They're hooting Montfleury!
BELLEROSE: [solemnly] Sic transit!† [to the porters] Sweep up and close every-
    thing down, but leave the lights on. We'll take dinner, but later we must
    return to rehearse tomorrow's farce.

[JODELET and BELLEROSE go out, bowing low to CYRANO.]

PORTER: [to CYRANO] You do not dine, Sir?
CYRANO: No.

[The PORTER goes out.]

LE BRET: Because?
CYRANO: [proudly] Because…[changing his tone as the PORTER goes away] I
    have no money!
LE BRET: [with the action of throwing a bag] But how's that? What about that
    bag of money?
CYRANO: My inheritance—all spent in one day!
LE BRET: How are you going to live for the next month?
CYRANO: I have nothing left.
LE BRET: How foolish of you to throw it all away like that!
CYRANO: But what a graceful action! Just think of it!
BUFFET-GIRL: [coughing, behind her counter] Ahem! [CYRANO and LE BRET
    turn. She comes timidly forward.] Sir, my heart cannot stand to hear that
    you are not eating. [showing the buffet] Please take what you like!
CYRANO: [taking off his hat] Gentle child, although my Gascon pride for-
    bids me to take the least bit of food from you, my fear of offending you

outweighs that pride. I will accept [*He goes over to the buffet.*]…one of these grapes. [*She offers him the whole bunch. He takes one.*] No, just one! [*She tries to give him wine, but he stops her.*] No, a glass of water will be just fine, and half a macaroon!

[*He puts back the other half.*]

LE BRET: What foolery!
BUFFET-GIRL: Please take something else!
CYRANO: I take your hand to kiss.

[*He kisses her hand as though she were a princess.*]

BUFFET-GIRL: Thank you, kind Sir! [*curtsying*] Good-night.

[*She goes out.*]

Scene v

CYRANO *and* LE BRET.

CYRANO: [*to* LE BRET] Now go ahead and talk. I'll listen now. [*He stands at the buffet and places before him first the macaroon.*] Dinner! [*then the grapes*] Dessert! [*then the glass of water*] Wine! [*He seats himself.*] So! And now to dine! Oh, I was so hungry, my friend—ravenous! [*He eats.*] You were saying—?
LE BRET: You must stop paying heed to these fools! They'll have you ruined! Ask a real friend and he'll tell you the truth about the effects of your arrogant behavior!
CYRANO: [*finishing his macaroon*] Enormous!
LE BRET: The Cardinal—
CYRANO: [*radiant*] The Cardinal was there?
LE BRET: He must have thought it—
CYRANO: Original, I'm sure!
LE BRET: But—
CYRANO: He's an author. It could not have failed to please him that I disrupted another author's play.
LE BRET: You make too many enemies!
CYRANO: [*eating his grapes*] How many do you think I've made tonight?
LE BRET: Forty, no less, not counting ladies.
CYRANO: Count them for me!

LE BRET: Well, Montfleury first, then the burgher, then de Guiche, de Valvert, Baro, the Academy—

CYRANO: Enough! I am overjoyed!

LE BRET: But I don't understand your behavior. Why do you live this way? Where will it lead you, in the end?

CYRANO: I wandered in a maze for many years. I was lost, and there were so many paths to choose. So I took…

LE BRET: Which?

CYRANO: I took the simplest path, by far! I decided to be admirable in everything!

LE BRET: [*shrugging his shoulders*] So you say. But what is the reason for your hate of Montfleury? Please tell me.

CYRANO: [*rising*] That lout! Rude and fat, but still thinks he's a danger to the ladies! While he's up there on stage sputtering out his part, he makes sheep's eyes at their boxes! I've hated him ever since the evening he presumed to raise his eyes to hers. When he did so, it was like seeing a slug crawl across a flower's petals!

LE BRET: [*stupefied*] How now? What? Can it be?

CYRANO: [*laughing bitterly*] That I should love? [*changing his tone, gravely*] I love.

LE BRET: But whom? You've never said!

CYRANO: Think for a minute! This nose of mine, which pokes out a quarter-mile ahead of me wherever I go, prevents me from being loved by even the poorest and most graceless of ladies. So who would I be in love with, then? The fairest of all ladies, of course. How could it be otherwise?

LE BRET: The fairest?

CYRANO: Oh yes, the fairest in the world. The most brilliant, the most refined, the most beautiful, the most golden-haired!

LE BRET: Who is this lady?

CYRANO: She is a mortal danger to all men. She is beautiful without knowing it, and possesses charms that she's not even aware of. She is like a trap set by nature—a sweet perfumed rose in whose petals Cupid† lurks in ambush! Anyone who has seen her smile has known perfection. She instills grace in every common thing and divinity in every careless gesture. Venus† in her shell was never so lovely, and Diana† in the forest never so graceful as my Lady when she strides through Paris!

LE BRET: Yes! Now I know! It's becoming quite clear!

CYRANO: Yes, quite transparent.

LE BRET: Your cousin, Madeleine Robin?

CYRANO: Roxane!

LE BRET: You love her! Then tell her so! She saw you triumph here this very night!

CYRANO: Look at me! Look at me and tell me what hope I can have with this vile protuberance! I am under no illusions about it, yet sometimes I am weak. Sometimes in the dim hours of the evening, I enter some fair sweet-smelling garden. With my poor ugly devil of a nose I smell spring's essence. In the silver rays of the moonlight I see some knight with a lady on his arm. And then I think "Oh, how lovely it would be to saunter through such a garden with my lady." My thoughts soar to ecstasy, but then they suddenly fall—when I see the shadow of my profile on the wall!

LE BRET: [*tenderly*] My friend!

CYRANO: Oh, my friend, at times it is very hard for me, and I cannot help but feel bitter. Sometimes, I feel so ugly and so all alone. Sometimes…

LE BRET: [*taking his hand*] You weep?

CYRANO: No, never! Think how unsuitable this nose is for a tear's path! I will never let the divine beauty of tears be connected to such common ugly grossness. There is nothing more solemn and sublime than a tear. If I were to weep, the grave emotion that a tear represents would turn to laughter and ridicule. And I will never let that happen!

LE BRET: Don't be sad! What is love but a game of chance?

CYRANO: [*shaking his head*] Do I look like a Caesar fit to woo Cleopatra?[†] Or a Tito to win Berenice?[†]

LE BRET: But you have great courage and wit! Think of the little maid who offered you food and drink just now. She was not repulsed by you at all! You must admit this!

CYRANO: [*impressed*] True!

LE BRET: See, then? And Roxane herself was death-pale as she watched the duel.

CYRANO: Pale?

LE BRET: You've already caught her heart and her fancy! Speak to her!

CYRANO: So that she can mock my face? That's the only thing on earth I fear!

PORTER: [*introducing someone to* CYRANO] Sir, someone is asking for you.

CYRANO: [*seeing the* DUENNA] My God! It's her duenna!

Scene vi

CYRANO, LE BRET *and the* DUENNA.

DUENNA: [*with a low bow*] I was asked to find out where a certain lady could see her heroic cousin in private.

CYRANO: [*overwhelmed*] See me?

DUENNA: [*curtsying*] Yes, Sir. She has some things to tell you.

CYRANO: Some things to…
DUENNA: [*still curtsying*] Yes, Sir, private matters.
CYRANO: [*staggering*] Ah, my God!
DUENNA: Early tomorrow morning, we will go to hear mass at Saint-Roch.
CYRANO: [*leaning against* LE BRET] My God!
DUENNA: And after mass, where can we meet you for a talk?
CYRANO: [*confused*] Where? Ah! My God!
DUENNA: Please name a place, Sir.
CYRANO: I'm thinking…
DUENNA: Where?
CYRANO: Ragueneau's bakery!
DUENNA: Where is his shop?
CYRANO: It's on the—on the—My God!—the Rue St. Honore.
DUENNA: [*going*] Good. We'll see you there at seven.
CYRANO: I will be there.

[*The* DUENNA *goes out.*]

Scene vii

CYRANO, LE BRET. *Then* ACTORS, ACTRESSES, CUIGY, BRISSAILLE, LIGNIERE, *the* PORTER, *the* VIOLINISTS.

CYRANO: [*falling into* LE BRET'S *arms*] A rendezvous! From her!
LE BRET: You're sad no more!
CYRANO: Ah! Whatever happens, at least she knows that I exist!
LE BRET: Now you'll be calm, I hope?
CYRANO: [*beside himself with joy*] Calm? You think I can be calm now? I'll be frenetic, frantic, raving mad! Oh, for an army to attack! I've got ten hearts in my breast and twenty arms at my sides. No more fighting with dwarfs! [*gesturing wildly*] No, I must fight giants now!

[*For a few moments the shadows of the actors have been moving on the stage, whispers are heard, the rehearsal is beginning. The* VIOLINISTS *are in their places.*]

A VOICE: Hello there! Silence, please! We're rehearsing now!
CYRANO: [*laughing*] We shall go!

[*He moves away. By the big door enter* CUIGY, BRISSAILLE, *and some* OFFICERS, *holding up* LIGNIERE, *who is drunk.*]

CUIGY: Cyrano!

CYRANO: What is it?

CUIGY: We've brought your friend, the drunken songbird.

CYRANO: [*recognizing him*] Ligniere! What has happened?

CUIGY: He's been looking for you.

BRISSAILLE: He doesn't dare to go home!

CYRANO: Why not?

LIGNIERE: [*in a husky voice, showing him a crumpled letter*] This letter warns
me—a hundred men out for me—revenge for that song I wrote—waiting for me at the Porte de Nesle—I must pass there in order to get
home—I dare not!—Please, let me sleep under your roof tonight!

CYRANO: A hundred men? You'll sleep in your own bed tonight!

LIGNIERE: [*frightened*] But—

CYRANO: [*in a fierce voice, showing him the lighted lantern held by the* PORTER,
who is listening curiously] Take the lantern. [LIGNIERE *grabs it.*] Let us
start! I swear that I will make your bed tonight myself! [*to the* OFFICERS]
Follow us! But stay behind—I only need you as witnesses!

CUIGY: A hundred men!

CYRANO: Any less would be too few!

[*The* ACTORS *and* ACTRESSES, *in their costumes, have come down from the stage,
and are listening.*]

LE BRET: But why get yourself involved in this mess?

CYRANO: Le Bret scolds again!

LE BRET: Why risk your life for that worthless drunkard?

CYRANO: [*slapping* LIGNIERE *on the shoulder*]
I'll tell you why. This wine-barrel of a man, this walking cask of
Burgundy, did an action one day that was full of grace. As he was leaving church, he saw his love taking holy water. He, who can't even stand
the sight of water, ran quickly to the basin, and drank it all, to the last
drop!

AN ACTRESS: Oh, what a graceful thing to do!

CYRANO: Indeed, was it not?

ACTRESS: [*to the others*] But why a hundred men against one poor poet?

CYRANO: Let's go! [*to the* OFFICERS] Gentlemen, when you see me charge,
give me no help, no matter what the odds!

ANOTHER ACTRESS: [*jumping from the stage*] Oh! I shall come and see!

ANOTHER: [*to an older* ACTOR, *while jumping down from the stage*] And you?

CYRANO: Come all—the Doctor, Isabel, Leander—everyone must come!
You'll form a madcap and motley group to add a little Italian farce to
this Spanish drama!

ALL THE WOMEN: [*dancing for joy*] Bravo!—Let's go!—My cloak!—Quick, my hood!

JODELET: Come on!

CYRANO: Play us a march, gentlemen of the band! [*The* VIOLINISTS *join the procession, which is forming. They take the footlights, and divide them for torches.*] Brave officers first! Next, women in costume! And twenty paces in front [*He takes his place.*] I alone! I, beneath my hat which glory itself has decorated, proud as Scipio!† Remember now, I forbid you to give me any aid! One, two, three! Open wide the doors! [*The* PORTER *opens the doors; a view of old Paris in the moonlight is seen.*] Ah! Paris wrapped in night, half nebulous, the moonlight streaming over the roof-tops! What a lovely frame for this wild battle scene! Beneath the haze, the Seine† trembles, mysterious, like a magic mirror. Soon you shall see what you shall see!

ALL: To the Porte de Nesle!

CYRANO: [*standing on the threshold*] Yes, to the Porte de Nesle! [*turning to the* ACTRESS] Did you not ask, young lady, why one hundred men are after this one poet? [*He draws his sword and then speaks calmly.*] It's because they know he's a friend of mine.

[*He goes out.* LIGNIERE *staggers first after him. The* ACTRESSES *then go out on the* OFFICERS' *arms, and then the actors go out. The procession starts to the sound of the violins and in the faint light of the candles.*]

CURTAIN.

ACT II

THE POET'S EATING-HOUSE

RAGUENEAU'S *pastry shop* It is a large kitchen at the corner of the Rue St. Honore and the Rue de l'Arbre Sec, which are seen in the background through the glass door, in the gray dawn.

On the left, in the foreground, is a counter. Above this counter hang geese, ducks, and water peacocks. In great china vases are tall bouquets of simple flowers, mainly yellow sunflowers.

On the same side, farther back, is a large open fireplace. From each andiron hangs a little saucepan. Drippings from various roasts fall into the pans.

There is a door in the right foreground. Farther back, a staircase leads to a little room under the roof, the entrance of which is visible through the open shutter. In this room a table is laid. A small candelabra is lit. It is a place for eating and drinking. A wooden gallery, continuing the staircase, apparently leads to other similar little rooms.

In the middle of the shop an iron hoop is suspended from the ceiling by a string with which it can be drawn up and down. Big game is hung around this hoop.

The ovens in the darkness under the stairs give forth a red glow. The copper pans shine. The spits are turning. Heaps of food are formed into pyramids. Hams are suspended from hooks. Scullions, fat cooks, and diminutive apprentices bustle and hurry around, their caps decorated with chicken feathers and hens' wings. On metal and wicker plates they bring in piles of cakes and tarts.

Tables are covered with rolls and dishes of food. Other tables surrounded with chairs are ready for the customers. RAGUENEAU *is seated at a small table which is covered with papers.*

THE CURTAIN RISES.

Scene i

RAGUENEAU, PASTRY-COOKS, *then* LISE. RAGUENEAU *is writing, with an inspired air, at a small table, and counting on his fingers.*

FIRST PASTRY-COOK: [*bringing in an elaborate fancy dish*] Fruits in nougat!

SECOND PASTRY-COOK: [*bringing another dish*] Custard!

THIRD PASTRY-COOK: [*bringing a roast, decorated with feathers*] Peacock!

FOURTH PASTRY-COOK: [*bringing a batch of cakes on a slab*] Cakes!

FIFTH PASTRY-COOK: [*bringing a sort of pie-dish*] Beef casserole!

RAGUENEAU: [*stopping his writing and raising his head*] The silver rays of the dawn begin to glint even now on the copper pans! Stifle the God of Song in your breast, Ragueneau! Soon the hour of the lute will come. But now, 'tis the hour of the oven! [*He rises, and speaks to one of the cooks.*] Improve that sauce—it's short of something!

COOK: How much too short?

RAGUENEAU: About three feet.

[*He passes on farther.*]

COOK: What on earth is he talking about?

FIRST COOK: [*showing a dish to* RAGUENEAU] The tart!

SECOND COOK: The pie!

RAGUENEAU: [*before the fire*] Retire, my muse, lest thy bright eyes be burned by the fire's blaze! [*to a* COOK, *showing him some loaves of bread*] You have split these loaves in the wrong place. Don't you know that the pause always occurs at the center of the line? [*to* ANOTHER, *showing him an unfinished pastry*] Build a roof for this palace of crust! [*to a young* APPRENTICE, *who is seated on the ground placing poultry on a spit*] On your spit, my son, you must alternate the modest chicken and the superb turkey, just as old Malherbe† alternated his long lines of verse with short ones. Just as a couplet should be well-turned, so should a roast!

ANOTHER APPRENTICE: [*coming up with a tray covered by a napkin*] Master, I thought of your tastes and made this. I hope it pleases you.

[*He uncovers the tray, and shows a large lyre made of pastry.*]

RAGUENEAU: [*enchanted*] A lyre!

APPRENTICE: 'Tis of pastry dough.

RAGUENEAU: [*touched*] With candied fruits!

APPRENTICE: And I made the strings out of sugar.

RAGUENEAU: [*giving him a coin*] Go, and drink to my health! [*seeing* LISE *enter*] Shhh! My wife! Go now, and hide that money! [*to* LISE, *showing her the lyre, with a self-conscious look*] Isn't it beautiful?

LISE: It's ridiculous!

[*She puts a pile of papers on the counter.*]

RAGUENEAU: Bags? Good! We need them! [*He looks at them.*] Heavens! My cherished pages! The poems of my friends! Torn apart to make bags for holding biscuits and cakes! You've desecrated great poetry, just as the Bacchantes tore apart Orpheus!†

LISE: [*dryly*] And am I not free to put to some use the only things that your wretched scribblers leave behind them by way of payment?

RAGUENEAU: Groveling ant! Don't insult the divine grasshoppers!

LISE: You never called your wife an ant—much less Bacchantes—until you started keeping company with that bunch!

RAGUENEAU: Oh, to turn my poetic words to such use!

LISE: That's all your poetry is good for!

RAGUENEAU: I hate to think of what you would do to prose, then!

Scene ii

The same, plus two CHILDREN, *who have just trotted into the shop.*

RAGUENEAU: What would you like, little ones?

FIRST CHILD: Three pies.

RAGUENEAU: [*serving them*] See, hot and well-browned.

SECOND CHILD: If you don't mind, Sir, will you wrap them up for us?

RAGUENEAU: [*aside*] Alas! One of my bags! [*to the* CHILDREN] Must I really wrap them up for you? [*He takes a bag, and just as he is about to put in the pies, he reads.*] "Ulysses thus, on leaving fair Penelope†..." No! Not that one! [*He puts it aside, and takes another, and as he is about to put in the pies, he reads.*] "The gold-locked Phoebus..." No! Not that one either!

LISE: [*impatiently*] What are you dallying for?

RAGUENEAU: Here! Here! [*He chooses a third, resignedly.*] The sonnet to Phillis! Oh, but it's also hard to part with!

LISE: Thank goodness he's made up his mind at last! [*shrugging her shoulders*] Fool!

[*She stands on a chair and begins to put plates on a shelf.*]

RAGUENEAU: [*taking advantage of the moment she turns her back, calls back the* CHILDREN, *who are already at the door*] Psst! Children! Give me back that sonnet and I'll give you six pies instead of three!

[*The* CHILDREN *give him back the bag, grab the pies, and go out.*]

RAGUENEAU: [*smoothing out the paper, begins to declaim*] "Phillis!..." Oh, a smear of butter on that sweet name! "Phillis!..."

[*Cyrano enters hurriedly.*]

Scene iii

RAGUENEAU, LISE, CYRANO, *then the* MUSKETEER.

CYRANO: What time is it?

RAGUENEAU: [*bowing low*] Six o'clock.

CYRANO: [*with emotion*] In just one hour's time!

[*He paces up and down the shop.*]

RAGUENEAU: [*following him*] Bravo! I saw the—

CYRANO: You saw what?

RAGUENEAU: Your duel!

CYRANO: Which one?

RAGUENEAU: Last night, or course, in the Hotel Burgundy!

CYRANO: [*contemptuously*] Oh, that duel...

RAGUENEAU: [*admiringly*] Indeed, the duel in verse!

LISE: He can't talk of anything else!

CYRANO: Well, fine! Let it be!

RAGUENEAU: [*lunging with a spit as if it is a sword*] "At the end of the refrain, I strike!...At the end of the refrain, I strike!"...Oh, it was wonderful! [*with increasing enthusiasm*] "At the end of the refrain—"

CYRANO: What time is it now, Ragueneau?

RAGUENEAU: [*stopping short in the act of thrusting to look at the clock*] Five minutes after six!…"I strike!" [*He straightens himself.*] Oh, to write a ballade!

LISE: [*to* CYRANO, *who has absently shaken hands with her as he passes the counter*] What's wrong with your hand?

CYRANO: Nothing, just a little cut.

RAGUENEAU: Have you been in some danger?

CYRANO: None at all.

LISE: [*shaking her finger at him*] I think you're lying when you say that!

CYRANO: Why? Did you see my nose quiver when I spoke? My goodness, it must have been a monstrous lie to be able to move it! [*changing his tone*] I'm waiting for someone. Please, when it comes time, leave us alone.

RAGUENEAU: But that's impossible! My poets are coming!

LISE: [*sarcastically*] Oh, indeed, for their first meal of the day!

CYRANO: I beg you, please take them aside when I make a signal for you to do so. What time is it now?

RAGUENEAU: Ten minutes after six.

CYRANO: [*nervously seating himself at* RAGUENEAU'S *table, and drawing some paper toward him*] A pen!

RAGUENEAU: [*giving him the one from behind his ear*] Here's a swan's quill.

A MUSKETEER: [*with fierce mustache, enters, and speaks in a very loud voice*] Good day!

[LISE *goes up to him quickly.*]

CYRANO: [*turning around*] Who's that?

RAGUENEAU: 'Tis a friend of my wife. A great warrior—or so he says himself.

CYRANO: [*taking up the pen, and motioning* RAGUENEAU *away*] Hush! [*to himself*] I'll write her a note, fold it, give it to her, and run out! [*throws down the pen*] Coward! But I just don't dare speak to her—not even one word! [*to* RAGUENEAU] What time is it?

RAGUENEAU: A quarter after six!

CYRANO: [*striking his chest*] I dare not speak a single word of all those I have in here! Writing it all down is much easier. [*He takes up the pen.*] I'll do it! I'll write her that love letter that is always in my thoughts! I've written it and rewritten it so many times that it lies there in my mind ready to be put down in pen and ink. All I must do is lay my soul beside this sheet of paper and copy what's written on it!

[*He writes. Through the glass of the door, the silhouettes of their figures move uncertainly and hesitatingly.*]

Scene iv

RAGUENEAU, LISE, *the* MUSKETEER. CYRANO *at the little table writing. The* POETS, *dressed in black, their stockings sagging and covered with mud.*

LISE: [*entering, to* RAGUENEAU] Here they come, your mud-spattered friends!

FIRST POET: [*entering, to* RAGUENEAU] Brother in art!

SECOND POET: [*to* RAGUENEAU, *shaking his hand*] Dear brother!

THIRD POET: High soaring eagle among pastry-cooks! [*He sniffs.*] My, it smells good here in your nest!

FOURTH POET: Phoebus of the kitchen!

FIFTH POET: Apollo† of cooks!

RAGUENEAU: [*whom they surround and embrace*] Ah! How quickly at ease I find myself among these friends!

FIRST POET: We were delayed by the mob; they're all crowded around the Porte de Nesle!

SECOND POET: Eight bandits lay dead in the street there—all slit open with sword-gashes!

CYRANO: [*raising his head a minute*] Eight? I thought it was seven.

[*He goes on writing.*]

RAGUENEAU: [*to* CYRANO] Do you know who the hero of that fight might be?

CYRANO: [*carelessly*] Not I.

LISE: [*to the* MUSKETEER] And you? Do you know?

MUSKETEER: [*twirling his mustache*] Maybe!

CYRANO: [*still writing, he is heard murmuring a word from time to time.*] "I love you!"

FIRST POET: 'Twas one man, they say. They all swear to it—just one man, who single-handedly beat the entire band of assassins!

SECOND POET: 'Twas a strange sight! Pikes and cudgels were strewn all over the ground!

CYRANO: [*writing*] "Your eyes…"

THIRD POET: They were picking up hats seven blocks away!

FIRST POET: My God! The man must have been ferocious!

CYRANO: [*still writing*] "Your lips…"

FIRST POET: He must have been a fearsome giant!

CYRANO: "…and when I see you come, I faint from fear."

SECOND POET: [*filching a cake*] What have you written lately, Ragueneau?

CYRANO: [*still writing*] "I worship you…" [*He stops, just as he is about to sign, and gets up, slipping the letter into his jacket.*] No need to sign, since I'll give it to her myself.

RAGUENEAU: [*to* SECOND POET] I have put a recipe into verse.

THIRD POET: [*seating himself by a plate of cream-puffs*] Go to it! Let's hear those verses!

FOURTH POET: [*looking at a cake which he has taken*] Oh my, this cake is lopsided! I'll fix it! [*He takes a bite off the top.*]

FIRST POET: [*taking a cake*] Ah, how this gingerbread woos the starving poet with its almond eyes!

SECOND POET: [*to* RAGUENEAU] Go ahead, we're listening.

THIRD POET: [*gently squeezing a cream-puff*] How it laughs! Until its very cream runs over!

SECOND POET: [*biting a bit off the lyre-shaped pastry*] This is the first time in my life I've gotten any true nourishment from the lyre!

RAGUENEAU: [*who has cleared his throat, settled his cap, and struck a pose, in preparation to recite his poem*] A recipe in verse!

SECOND POET: [*to first, nudging him*] Is this your breakfast?

FIRST POET: [*to second*] Yes, and you are taking your dinner, it seems.

RAGUENEAU: How almond tartlets are made.

> Beat your eggs up, light and quick;
> Froth them thick;
> Mingle with them while you beat
> Juice of lemon, essence fine;
> Then combine
> The burst milk of almonds sweet.
>
> Circle with a custard paste
> The slim waist
> Of your tartlet-molds; the top
> With a skillful finger print,
> Nick and dint,
> Round the edge, then, drop by drop,
> Pour some cream upon each one—
> Almost done!
> In the oven place each mold.
> Reappearing, softly browned,
> The renowned
> Almond tartlets you behold!

THE POETS: [*with mouths crammed full*] Exquisite! Delicious!

A POET: [*choking*] Humph!

[*They go upstage, still eating.*]

CYRANO: [*who has been watching, goes toward* RAGUENEAU] Don't you see how they stuff themselves while you recite your poetry?

RAGUENEAU: [*in a low voice, smiling*] Oh, yes! I see it well enough, but I won't let them know that I see it. I wouldn't want to embarrass them, you know. Plus, I gain a double pleasure when I recite my poems to them, for I give those poor starving fellows the freedom to eat, even while I gratify my own dearest weakness!

CYRANO: [*clapping him on the shoulder*] Friend, I like you! [RAGUENEAU *goes after his friends.* CYRANO *follows him with his eyes, and then speaks rather sharply.*] Lise! Is that musketeer making passes at you?

LISE: [*offended*] One proud glance of my eye can conquer any man that should dare venture to attack my virtue!

CYRANO: Pooh! Conquering eyes, I think, are often conquered eyes.

LISE: [*choking with anger*] But—

CYRANO: [*bluntly*] I like Ragueneau. So mark my words, Lise—I will not permit you to make a laughing-stock of him by any—

LISE: But—

CYRANO: [*who has raised his voice so as to be heard by the* MUSKETEER] A word to the wise...

[*He bows to the* MUSKETEER *and goes to the doorway to watch, after looking at the clock.*]

LISE: [*to the* MUSKETEER, *who has merely bowed in answer to* CYRANO'S *bow*] What's with you? Have you no courage? You didn't even make fun of his nose!

MUSKETEER: His nose? Oh yes, his nose.

[*He goes quickly farther away, and* LISE *follows him.*]

CYRANO: [*from the doorway, signing to* RAGUENEAU *to take the poets away*] Psst!

RAGUENEAU: [*showing them the door on the right*] We shall have more privacy in here.

CYRANO: [*impatiently*] Psst! Psst!

RAGUENEAU: [*drawing them farther away*]
We can better read our poetry over here.

FIRST POET: [*despairingly, with his mouth full*] What! Must we leave the cakes?

SECOND POET: Never! Let's take them with us!

[*They all go out behind* RAGUENEAU, *after sweeping all the cakes off the trays.*]

Scene v

CYRANO, ROXANE, *the* DUENNA.

CYRANO: Ah! If I see even the faintest glimmer of hope, I'll give her my letter! [ROXANE, *masked, followed by the* DUENNA, *appears at the glass pane of the door. He opens it quickly.*] Come in! [*aside to the* DUENNA] May I have two words with you?

DUENNA: You may have as many as you like, Sir!

CYRANO: Are you fond of sweet things?

DUENNA: Oh, yes, I could eat myself sick with them!

CYRANO: [*grabbing some of the paper bags from the counter*] Good. Take these two sonnets written by Monsieur Benserade†—

DUENNA: [*slightly disappointed*] Oh...

CYRANO: Which I will fill for you with cream cakes!

DUENNA: [*changing her expression*] Oh!

CYRANO: I'll wrap up six of them for you in the bosom of a poem by Saint Amant!† And here in these verses of Chapelain† I'll drop a piece of sponge cake. Oh, and do you like warm pies?

DUENNA: Oh, yes, to the core of my heart!

CYRANO: [*filling her arms with the bags*] Now, please go and enjoy them all out in the street.

DUENNA: But—

[*He shuts the door, comes down toward* ROXANE, *and stands at a respectful distance from her with his hat in his hand.*]

Scene vi

CYRANO, ROXANE

CYRANO: Blessed be this day that you recognize my existence and come to meet me, and to say...

ROXANE: [*who has taken off her mask*] I came to say thank you, first of all, for your victory last night. That arrogant man whom you beat in swordplay was the man whom a certain great lord, infatuated with me—

CYRANO: de Guiche?

ROXANE: [*casting her eyes downward*] —tried to force on me as a husband.

CYRANO: Indeed, a husband! A duped husband! A husband only in form!
[*bowing*] Then I am glad to know that I fought last night not for my ugly
nose but for your beautiful virtue!

ROXANE: I also have a confession to make. But before I do so, I must see you
again as that brother-friend with whom I used to play by the lakeside!

CYRANO: Yes, you would come each spring to Bergerac!

ROXANE: Remember the reeds you used to cut to make your swords?

CYRANO: And you wove corn silk to make braids for your dolls' hair!

ROXANE: Those were the days of games!

CYRANO: And eating blackberries!

ROXANE: In those days, you did everything I asked of you!

CYRANO: You were called Madeleine then, in your little girl dress!

ROXANE: Was I pretty then?

CYRANO: You certainly were not plain!

ROXANE: I remember many times you would come running to me, hands all
cut up from a fall, and I would act as if I were your mother. I would try
to sound severe. [*She takes his hand.*] I'd say sternly, "What happened
here? Did you hurt yourself again?" [*She looks at his hand, surprised.*]
Oh! It's too much! What happened to your hand? [CYRANO *tries to draw
away his hand.*] No, let me see! Still injuring yourself, at your age!
Where did you get that scratch?

CYRANO: I got it while playing at the Porte de Nesle.

ROXANE: [*seating herself by the table, and dipping her handkerchief in a glass
of water*] Give me your hand!

CYRANO: [*sitting by her*] So soft! So motherly and sweet!

ROXANE: Tell me, while I wipe away the blood, how many men were against
you?

CYRANO: Oh, about a hundred.

ROXANE: Tell me more!

CYRANO: No, let it be. But I'd like you to tell me what it was you were about
to confess.

ROXANE: [*keeping his hand*] Yes, now I can tell you! The memory of those old
days makes me bolder! Here it is. I am in love with someone.

CYRANO: Ah!

ROXANE: But he does not know it.

CYRANO: Ah!

ROXANE: Not yet.

CYRANO: Ah!

ROXANE: But he shall soon learn.

CYRANO: Ah!

ROXANE: A poor young man, who all this time has loved me, timidly, from
afar, and dares not speak.

CYRANO: Ah!

ROXANE: My, your hand feels feverish! He dares not speak, but I have seen love trembling on his lips.

CYRANO: Ah!

ROXANE: [*bandaging his hand with her handkerchief*] And it just so happens, dear cousin, that he's a member of your regiment!

CYRANO: Ah!

ROXANE: [*laughing*] A cadet in your own company!

CYRANO: Ah!

ROXANE: His brow bears the stamp of genius. He is proud, noble, young, intrepid, handsome—

CYRANO: [*rising suddenly, very pale*] Handsome!

ROXANE: What's the matter?

CYRANO: Nothing. It's... [*showing his hand, smiling*] It's only a little pain from this scratch!

ROXANE: I love him. Now I've said it. But I must tell you I've only seen him at the theater.

CYRANO: You mean you've never spoken to him?

ROXANE: Eyes can speak.

CYRANO: But then, how do you know that he...?

ROXANE: Oh, people talk. Gossip spreads quickly under the linden trees at Place Royale.

CYRANO: He is a cadet?

ROXANE: Yes, in the Guards

CYRANO: What's his name?

ROXANE: Baron Christian de Neuvillette.

CYRANO: What? He's not in the Guards.

ROXANE: He just joined this morning, under Captain Carbon de Castel-Jaloux.

CYRANO: Oh, how quickly we lose our hearts! But, my poor child—

DUENNA: [*opening the door*] I've eaten all the cakes, Monsieur Bergerac!

CYRANO: Then read the poems printed on the bags! [*She goes out.*] My poor child, you who love flowing words and sharp wit—what if he turns out to be dull?

ROXANE: No, his hair is just like the hair of one of d'Urfe's heroes!†

CYRANO: Ah! Nice hair but witless speech, perhaps?

ROXANE: Oh, no! His words are fair and elegant—I can just feel it!

CYRANO: All words seem elegant when they lurk beneath an elegant mustache! Suppose he's really a fool!

ROXANE: [*stamping her foot*] Then I'll just die!

CYRANO: [*after a pause*] Did you bring me here in order to tell me this? I must say I don't understand why.

ROXANE: It's because I learned just yesterday that all of your company are Gascons and—

CYRANO: And we always provoke any newcomer who somehow gains favor without being a pure Gascon?

ROXANE: Yes! Think how I fear for him!

CYRANO: [aside] And with good reason!

ROXANE: But when I saw you last night, fighting so bravely and fearlessly, holding your own against all of those brutes, I thought, "If only he, whom everyone fears, if only he would…"

CYRANO: All right. I will befriend your little Baron.

ROXANE: Oh! Do you promise you'll do this for me? I've always held you as a tender friend.

CYRANO: Yes, yes.

ROXANE: Then you will be his friend?

CYRANO: I swear!

ROXANE: And he shall fight no duels?

CYRANO: None. I promise.

ROXANE: You are so kind, cousin! Now I must go. [She puts on her mask and veil, and then speaks distractedly.] Oh, but you haven't told me about your battle last night—what a hero you must have been! Please tell him to write to me! [She sends him a kiss with her fingers.] Oh, how good you are!

CYRANO: Yes, yes.

ROXANE: A hundred men against you! What a hero! But I must go. You're such a great friend!

CYRANO: Yes, yes.

ROXANE: Tell him to write to me. You'll tell me all about the fight one day. A hundred men! Oh, how brave!

CYRANO: [bowing to her] I have fought better since.

[She goes out. CYRANO stands motionless, with his eyes to the ground. There is a silence. The door opens and RAGUENEAU looks in.]

Scene vii

CYRANO, RAGUENEAU, the POETS, CARBON DE CASTEL-JALOUX, the CADETS, a CROWD, then DE GUICHE.

RAGUENEAU: Can we come in?

CYRANO: [motionless] Yes.

[RAGUENEAU *signals to his friends and they all come in. At the same time, by a door at the back,* CARBON DE CASTEL-JALOUX *enters, in Captain's uniform. He makes gestures of surprise upon seeing* CYRANO.]

CARBON: Here he is!

CYRANO: [*raising his head*] Captain!

CARBON: [*delightedly*] Our hero! We heard all about it! Thirty or more of my cadets are here!

CYRANO: [*shrinking back*] But...

CARBON: [*trying to draw him away*] Come with me! They will not rest until they see you!

CYRANO: No!

CARBON: They're just across the street, drinking at The Bear's Head.

CYRANO: I—

CARBON: [*going to the door and calling across the street in a loud, booming voice*] He won't come! The hero's in a bad mood!

A VOICE: [*outside*] Sandious!†

[*There is a tumult outside. The noise of boots and swords is heard.*]

CARBON: [*rubbing his hands*] They're running across the street!

[*The cadets enter, shouting exclamations in the Gascon dialect.*]

RAGUENEAU: [*drawing back, startled*] Gentlemen, are you all from Gascony?

THE CADETS: Yes, all of us!

A CADET: [*to* CYRANO] Bravo!

CYRANO: [*nodding*] Baron!

ANOTHER: [*shaking his hands*] Hurrah!

CYRANO: Baron!

THIRD CADET: Come! I must embrace you!

CYRANO: Baron!

SEVERAL CADETS: We'll all embrace him! All in turn!

CYRANO: [*not knowing whom to reply to*] Baron—Baron—I beg you—

RAGUENEAU: Are you all Barons, Sirs?

CADETS: All of us!

RAGUENEAU: Is it true?

FIRST CADET: You could build a tower with nothing but our coronets!

LE BRET: [*entering, and running up to* CYRANO] Everyone wants to see you! There's a wild mob led by the men who followed you last night!

CYRANO: [*alarmed*] You haven't told them where to find me, have you?

LE BRET: [*rubbing his hands*] Yes!

A BURGHER: [entering, followed by a group of men] Sir, everyone in the
    Marais† is coming here!

[Outside the street has filled with people. Carriages are stopping.]

LE BRET: [in a low voice, smiling, to CYRANO] What happened with Roxane?
CYRANO: [quickly] Hush!
CROWD: [calling from outside] Cyrano!

[A CROWD rushes into the shop, pushing one another and cheering.]

RAGUENEAU: [standing on a table] My shop is being invaded! They're break-
    ing everything! How magnificent!
CROWD: [gathering around CYRANO] My friend! My friend!
CYRANO: It seems that just yesterday I didn't have this many friends!
LE BRET: [delighted] Success!
A YOUNG MARQUIS: [hurrying up with his hands held out] My friend, if you
    only knew—
CYRANO: Friend? How can you be my friend if I've never even seen you
    before?
ANOTHER: Sir, please let me present to you some fair ladies who are waiting
    in my carriage.
CYRANO: [coldly] Oh? And who will introduce me to you?
LE BRET: [astonished] What's wrong with you?
CYRANO: Hush!
A MAN OF LETTERS: [with a writing-board] Sir, may I have a few details?
CYRANO: No.
LE BRET: [nudging his elbow] That's Théophraste Renaudot, editor of the
    "Gazette!"†
CYRANO: Who cares?
LE BRET: But his paper is of great importance! They say it will be an
    immense success!
A POET: [advancing] Sir—
CYRANO: Another one!
POET: Please permit me to make a pentacrostic out of your name.
A MAN: [also advancing] Please, Sir—
CYRANO: Enough! Enough!

[There is a movement in the CROWD. DE GUICHE appears, escorted by OFFICERS,
including CUIGY, BRISSAILLE, and the officers who went with CYRANO the night
before. CUIGY comes rapidly up to CYRANO.]

CUIGY: [*to* CYRANO] I present Monsieur de Guiche. [*The* CROWD *murmurs and everyone gets out of the way.*] He comes with a message from the Marshal of Gassion!

DE GUICHE: [*bowing to* CYRANO] The Marshal expresses his admiration, Sir, for your exploit that everyone is talking about.

CROWD: Bravo!

CYRANO: [*bowing*] The Marshal is a judge of valor.

DE GUICHE: He could not have believed it, unless these gentlemen had sworn they witnessed it.

CUIGY: With our own eyes!

LE BRET: [*aside to* CYRANO, *who appears distracted*] Aren't you going to say something?

CYRANO: Hush!

LE BRET: What is it? You seem to be suffering.

CYRANO: [*starting*] Suffering? In front of this mob? [*He draws himself up, twirls his mustache, and throws back his shoulders.*] Wait! You shall see!

DE GUICHE: [*to whom* CUIGY *has spoken in a low voice*] Your career is already filled with great exploits. And you also serve with those crazy Gascons?

CYRANO: Yes, I'm with the Cadets.

A CADET: [*in a fierce tone*] He's one of us!

DE GUICHE: [*looking at the* CADETS, *who all stand behind* CYRANO] Ah! These proud and haughty gentlemen must be the famous warriors!

CARBON: Cyrano!

CYRANO: Yes, captain!

CARBON: Since all my company is assembled here, please favor me and present them to the Count.

CYRANO: [*making two steps toward* DE GUICHE *and pointing to the* CADETS] My Lord de Guiche, permit me to present my fellow cadets:

> The bold Cadets of Gascony,
> Of Carbon de Castel-Jaloux!
> Brawling and swaggering boastfully,
> The bold Cadets of Gascony!
> Bragging of arms and heraldry,
> Their veins brimming with blood so blue,
> The bold Cadets of Gascony,
> Of Carbon de Castel-Jaloux.
>
> Eagle-eyed, and graceful as cats,
> Fierce mustache and wolf-like grin,
> They slash those before them as though they were gnats.

Eagle-eyed, and graceful as cats,
Haphazardly sporting their torn and worn hats,
With feathers to cover the holes there within,
Eagle-eyed and graceful as cats,
Fierce mustache and wolf-like grin.

Stab-Your-Belly and Slit-Your-Trunk
Are the gentlest nicknames they bear.
With fame and glory their soul is drunk!
Stab-Your-Belly and Slit-Your-Trunk,
In brawl and battle they show their spunk,
Doing things others would never dare,
Stab-Your-Belly and Slit-Your-Trunk
Are the gentlest nicknames they bear!

Behold the Cadets of Gascony!
All jealous lovers are sport for you!
Fair ladies will lose their purity!
Behold the Cadets of Gascony!
The ones all husbands fear to see,
For their wives the Cadets will woo!
Behold the Cadets of Gascony!
Husbands and lovers are game for you!

DE GUICHE: [looking snobby and seated casually in an armchair brought quickly by RAGUENEAU] A poet! It's the latest fashion! Would you like to be my personal poet?

CYRANO: No, Sir! I'm no man's poet!

DE GUICHE: Your exploits last night pleased my uncle, Cardinal Richelieu. I'll gladly say a word to him for you.

LE BRET: [overjoyed] My God!

DE GUICHE: I believe you have written a play?

LE BRET: [in CYRANO'S ear] Your play! Agrippine† shall be performed at last!

DE GUICHE: Take it to him.

CYRANO: [beginning to be tempted and attracted] Well, I...

DE GUICHE: He is a skilled critic. He may correct a line or two, at most.

CYRANO: [whose face stiffens at once] Impossible! My blood freezes just to imagine that even one comma should be changed!

DE GUICHE: But when he likes a piece of writing, he pays extremely well for it, good friend.

CYRANO: He cannot pay as well as I do. For when a verse I've written pleases me, I pay the writer the highest reward by singing it to myself!

DE GUICHE: You are proud.

CYRANO: Really? Have you noticed that?

A CADET: [*entering, with a string of old battered plumed beaver hats, full of holes, slung on his word*] Look, Cyrano! See the brightly-feathered game we found this morning out in the street!

CARBON: The spoils of war!

ALL: [*laughing*] Ha, ha, ha!

CUIGY: Whoever hired those cowards must be cursing and swearing today!

BRISSAILLE: Who was it?

DE GUICHE: It was me. [*The laughter stops.*] The job was too dirty for my sword, so I hired them to punish that drunken sot of a poet.

[*A tense silence ensues.*]

CADET: [*in a low voice, to* CYRANO, *showing him the hats*] What should we do with them? They're all greasy. Maybe we should make a stew!

CYRANO: [*taking the sword and, with a salute, dropping the hats at* DE GUICHE'S *feet*] Please, Sir, be good enough to return them to your friends.

DE GUICHE: [*rising, and speaking sharply*] Bring me my chair at once! I'm leaving! [*to* CYRANO, *angrily*] As to you, Sir!

VOICE: [*in the street*] Porters! Bring Count de Guiche's chair!

DE GUICHE: [*who has regained control of himself, smiling*] Have you read *Don Quixote*?†

CYRANO: I have! And I take off my hat to that mad knight!

DE GUICHE: I advise you study—

PORTER: [*appearing at the back*] My lord's chair!

DE GUICHE: —the windmill chapter!

CYRANO: [*bowing*] Chapter thirteen.

DE GUICHE: For when one attacks windmills, it may happen that—

CYRANO: Are you saying that I attack those who change with every change of the breeze?

DE GUICHE: —that the arms of windmills may catch you and sweep you down into the mud!

CYRANO: Or upward to the stars!

[DE GUICHE *goes out and gets into his chair. The other* LORDS *go away whispering together.* LE BRET *goes to the door with them. The* CROWD *leaves.*]

Scene viii

CYRANO, LE BRET, *and the* CADETS, *who are eating and drinking at the tables on the right and left.*

CYRANO: [*bowing mockingly to those who go out without daring to salute him*]
Gentlemen…Gentlemen…

LE BRET: [*coming back, with an expression of despair*]
Oh, what a fine mess!

CYRANO: Oh, go ahead! Scold away!

LE BRET: You must admit that destroying every opportunity that comes your way is a little extreme!

CYRANO: Yes, I admit it. I am sometimes extreme.

LE BRET: [*triumphantly*] Ah!

CYRANO: But to take a stand, or to defend a principle, sometimes requires one to act in extreme ways.

LE BRET: Oh, lay aside your pride for a moment. Fortune and glory await you!

CYRANO: Oh, yes? But what would I have to do for it? Seek a patron to support me and protect me? Be like the wretched ivy that clings around a big tree and creeps upward not by its own strength but by trickery? No, thank you! Dedicate poems to bankers, like other poets have done? Act like a cringing fool just for the hope of seeing a condescending smile on a patron's lips? Thank you, but no! Learn to swallow insults every day? Scrape my knees raw from kneeling and bend my back till it breaks from bowing? No, thank you! Or be two-faced and sly, running with the hare while at the same time hunting with the hounds? Learn the cheap art of flattering people so that they may praise me? Step on people to make my way ahead? Navigate the sea of life with madrigals for sails, blown gently windward by old ladies' sighs? Thank you, but no! Bribe kindly editors to print my poetry? Aspire to be elected pope of tavern councils held by drunken idiots? Work my whole life to bank my reputation on one famous sonnet instead of writing hundreds? Be terrorized by all the papers, thinking such things as, "Oh, if only the *Mercury* would give me a kind review!" Grow pale and fearful and scheming? Prefer to make visits instead of poems? Seek introductions to the right people, sign the right petitions? No! No! And no again! But sing? And dream and laugh? Yes! Go freely, wherever I please, with eyes that look straight forward and with a fearless voice! To wear my hat just the way I choose! To decide for myself in any situation whether to fight a duel or to recite a poem! To work without one thought of fortune or fame, and to realize that journey to the moon! Never to write a line that has not sprung straight from my heart. To be modest. To be content with every flower, fruit or even leaf—but pluck them from my own garden and no one else's! And then, if glory ever does by chance come my way, I'll pay no tribute to Caesar,[†] because the merit will be my own. In short, I will never be like that wretched ivy. Whether I rise very high or not, I am content because I climb alone![†]

LE BRET: Be alone if you will, but where did you ever get the idea that you should be making enemies at every turn?

CYRANO: I got it from watching you make friends at every turn by fawning over people and flattering them. As you smile at people you despise, I pass by joyfully, thinking, "Oh, good—I've made another enemy today!"

LE BRET: Sheer lunacy!

CYRANO: Think of it as my vice. It gives me pleasure to displease people. I love to be hated! I march better beneath the crossfire of hostile glances! How amusing it is to see my jacket stained with so many spatters of envy and fear! The dull friendships which you and others keep enfold your neck like an open-laced collar. Such a collar makes it easy to move your head every which way, but makes it impossible to hold your head up straight. My hatred is like a stiff and starched collar which presses in upon me and keeps my head held high! And every new enemy adds a stiff new pleat to it, for hatred grips like a vice, but frames one like a halo!

LE BRET: [*after a silence, taking his arm*] Speak loud and proud to the world. But whisper the truth into my ear—she does not love you, does she?

CYRANO: [*sharply*] Hush!

[CHRISTIAN *has just entered, and has tried to mingle with the cadets, who do not speak to him. He has seated himself at a table, where* LISE *serves him.*]

Scene ix

CYRANO, LE BRET, *the* CADETS, CHRISTIAN DE NEUVILLETTE.

A CADET: [*seated at a table, glass in hand*] Cyrano! [CYRANO *turns around*] Tell the story!

CYRANO: Give me a moment!

[*He goes upstage, arm and arm with* LE BRET, *the two of them talking in low voices.*]

THE CADET: [*rising and coming downstage*] The story of the fight! [*He stops at the table where* CHRISTIAN *is seated.*] It will be a good lesson for this timid young apprentice!

CHRISTIAN: [*raising his head*] Apprentice?

ANOTHER CADET: Yes, you weak northerner!

CHRISTIAN: Weak?

FIRST CADET: [*mockingly*] Listen, Monsieur de Neuvillette, there is something you must know. There is an object that no one dares to name. Calling attention to this object would be like mentioning rope in a home where a man hung himself!

CHRISTIAN: What might this object be?

ANOTHER CADET: [*in a fierce voice*] See here! [*He taps his finger three times, mysteriously, on his nose.*] Do you understand?

CHRISTIAN: Oh! You must mean—

ANOTHER CADET: Hush! Never breathe that word, unless you want to deal with him!

[*He points to* CYRANO, *who is talking with* LE BRET.]

ANOTHER CADET: [*who has meanwhile come up quietly to sit on the table, whispering behind him*] Listen here! He put two men to death, just because they spoke with nasally voices!

ANOTHER: [*in a hollow voice, darting on all fours from under the table, where he had crept*] If you'd rather not die young, do not ever mention the fatal cartilage!

ANOTHER: [*clapping him on the shoulder*] Not a word! Not a gesture! Even pulling out a handkerchief could land you dead!

[*There is a silence. All the* CADETS *stand with crossed arms and look at* CHRISTIAN. *He rises and goes over to* CARBON DE CASTEL-JALOUX, *who is talking to an officer, and pretends to see nothing.*]

CHRISTIAN: Captain!

CARBON: [*turning and looking at him from head to foot*] Sir!

CHRISTIAN: Please tell me, what should one do to southerners who swagger and boast?

CARBON: Prove to them that one can be a northerner and also be brave!

[*He turns his back on him.*]

CHRISTIAN: Thank you.

FIRST CADET: [*to* CYRANO] Now tell the tale!

ALL: The tale!

CYRANO: [*coming toward them*]

The tale? [*They all bring their stools up and group around him, listening eagerly.* CHRISTIAN *sits astride a chair.*] Well! I went all alone to meet the scoundrels. The full moon was shining like a big clock in the sky. Suddenly, an unseen hand slipped a cloud in front of the clock face, and the night went black! All the docks were hidden in the murky dark. I could see nothing further—

CHRISTIAN: Than the end of your nose!

[*There is complete silence. Everyone slowly rises, looking in terror at* CYRANO, *who has stopped speaking, dumbfounded. There is a pause.*]

CYRANO: Who in God's name is that?

A CADET: [*whispering*] He just joined today.

CYRANO: [*making a step toward* CHRISTIAN] Today?

CARBON: [*in a low voice*] Yes, his name is Baron de Neuvil—

CYRANO: [*stopping himself*] Very well. [*He turns pale, then turns red, and looks as if he will attack* CHRISTIAN.] I— [*He gains control of himself.*] What was I saying? [*with a burst of rage*] MORDIOUS!† [*then continuing calmly*] It was dark. [*The* CADETS *are astonished. They reseat themselves, staring at him.*] On I went, thinking to myself, "For a brave cause, I might provoke some great man, some great prince, who might certainly break—"

CHRISTIAN: Your nose!

[*Everyone starts up.* CHRISTIAN *balances on his chair.*]

CYRANO: [*in a choked voice*] My teeth! Who might break my teeth, and that I, unwisely, might be putting my—

CHRISTIAN: Your nose!

CYRANO: Myself into a bad situation. He might prove strong and rap me—

CHRISTIAN: In the nose!

CYRANO: [*wiping his forehead*]

On the knuckles! But I said to myself, "Forward, Gascon! Duty calls! On, Cyrano!" And so I ventured on. And then, from out of the shadows, came—

CHRISTIAN: A crack on the nose!

CYRANO: A thrust from someone's sword! I parried it, and found myself—

CHRISTIAN: Nose to nose—

CYRANO: [*rushing at him*] Good God in heaven! [*All the Gascons leap up to see,* *but when he is close to* CHRISTIAN, *he controls himself and continues.*] With a hundred brutes, who all stank—

CHRISTIAN: So much you had to hold your nose!

CYRANO: [*ghostly pale, but smiling*] Of onions and cheap brandy! I leapt out and charged right into the midst of them—

CHRISTIAN: Nose first!

CYRANO: I charge! I immediately gore two and impale one! Then another aims at me—Paf!—and I parry—

CHRISTIAN: Pif!

CYRANO: [*bursting out loud*] Great God! Get out! All of you!

[*The* CADETS *rush to the doors.*]

FIRST CADET: The tiger awakens!

CYRANO: Everyone out! Leave me alone with him!

SECOND CADET: He'll be mince meat! Chopped up finely and ready to be baked into a pastry!

RAGUENEAU: I am turning pale! I curl up like a napkin, limp and white!

CARBON: Let's be gone.

A CADET: There won't be a crumb left of him!

ANOTHER: I die of fright just to think of what will happen to him!

ANOTHER: [*shutting the door as they all leave*] Something too horrible!

[*All have gone out by different doors; some have left by the staircase.* CYRANO *and* CHRISTIAN *are face to face, looking at each other for a moment.*]

Scene x

CYRANO, CHRISTIAN.

CYRANO: Embrace me!

CHRISTIAN: But, Sir—

CYRANO: You're a brave man.

CHRISTIAN: Oh! But—

CYRANO: I insist!

CHRISTIAN: Please tell me—

CYRANO: Come, embrace me! I'm her brother.

CHRISTIAN: Whose brother?

CYRANO: Roxane's!

CHRISTIAN: [*rushing up to him*] Oh, heavens! Her brother?

CYRANO: Cousin, brother—same thing!

CHRISTIAN: And has she told you…?

CYRANO: She's told me everything!

CHRISTIAN: Does she love me? Please tell me!

CYRANO: Maybe!

CHRISTIAN: [*taking his hands*] How glad I am to meet you, Sir!

CYRANO: Well, that's a rather sudden change in feeling!

CHRISTIAN: Please forgive me.

CYRANO: [*puts his hands on* CHRISTIAN'S *shoulders and looks at him*]
   It's true, you *are* a handsome rogue.

CHRISTIAN: Oh, Sir! If you only knew how much I admire you!

CYRANO: But what about all those 'noses?'

CHRISTIAN: Oh! I take them back!

CYRANO: Roxane expects a letter from you.

CHRISTIAN: Oh, woe is me!

CYRANO: What's wrong?

CHRISTIAN: If I open my mouth, I'm lost!

CYRANO: Why so?

CHRISTIAN: Because I'm a fool! Oh, I could die for shame!

CYRANO: If one calls himself a fool, he cannot really be a fool. Besides, you
   did not attack me like a fool.

CHRISTIAN: It's easy to find words to pick a fight. I'll admit I have a certain
   military wit. But before women, I'm at a loss! True, when I pass by
   them, their eyes are kind, but—

CYRANO: Aren't they even kinder when you stop?

CHRISTIAN: No! For I am one of those men who are tongue-tied. I don't know
   how to speak my love to a woman.

CYRANO: And, I, it seems, would be able to speak *my* love if only Nature had
   been kinder to me.

CHRISTIAN: Oh, to be able to express my thoughts with grace!

CYRANO: Oh, to be a musketeer, with a handsome face!

CHRISTIAN: Roxane is so intelligent. I'm sure to prove a disappointment
   to her!

CYRANO: [*looking at him*] If only I had a face like yours to speak what's in my
   soul!

CHRISTIAN: [*with despair*] If only I had some eloquence!

CYRANO: [*abruptly*] I'll lend you mine! If you'll lend me your handsome
   face! Blended together, we'll make one romantic hero!

CHRISTIAN: But how?

CYRANO: Do you think you can repeat whatever I may tell you?

CHRISTIAN: What do you mean?

CYRANO: Roxane will not be disillusioned if the two of us woo her as one!
   Let my words speak through your lips. Let my soul pass from this leather

jacket to your embroidered coat. We will win her together!†

CHRISTIAN: But, Cyrano—

CYRANO: Will you do it?

CHRISTIAN: I'm afraid!

CYRANO: You're afraid you will chill her heart if you speak to her yourself. But if you let me speak through your lips, her heart will flame!

CHRISTIAN: Your eyes are flashing!

CYRANO: Will you do it?

CHRISTIAN: Would it please you so?

CYRANO: [passionately] It would! [then calmly, business-like] It would... amuse me! It's the type of challenge every poet would hope for. Let us complete each other. You will march victorious, in the light, while I go in your shadow. Let me make you witty and intelligent, and you shall make me handsome!

CHRISTIAN: The letter! I could never—

CYRANO: [taking out the letter he had written] Here it is! Here's your letter!

CHRISTIAN: What?

CYRANO: Take it! All it needs is your signature.

CHRISTIAN: But I—

CYRANO: Do not fear. Go ahead and send it. It's entirely suitable.

CHRISTIAN: But how did you already—?

CYRANO: Oh! We poets always have our pockets full of love letters, written to so many imaginary beauties. Now, you can take this one and make the words ring true. Take this fictional letter, meant for no particular lady, and put it to real use. Take all my insincere romantic lines and give them a direction. Make it so these haphazard verses will come together and surround her like love birds coming home to nest!

CHRISTIAN: Should I change anything at all? If it wasn't written with Roxane in mind, then how will it fit her?

CYRANO: It will fit her like a glove!

CHRISTIAN: But—

CYRANO: Love believes anything! Roxane will think each word was inspired by herself!

CHRISTIAN: My friend!

[He throws himself into CYRANO's arms and they remain this way.]

Scene xi

CYRANO, CHRISTIAN, *the* GASCONS, *the* MUSKETEER, LISE.

A CADET: [*opening the door halfway*] Not a word! Such a deadly silence! I dare not look! [*He puts his head in.*] What's this!

ALL THE CADETS: [*entering, and seeing* CYRANO *and* CHRISTIAN *embracing*] Oh!

A CADET: This is unbelievable!

MUSKETEER: [*in a jeering tone*] Ho! Ho!

CARBON: Can it be that our demon has become a saint? When struck on one nostril, he turns the other?

MUSKETEER: Well then, I suppose it's safe to speak about his nose from now on! [*calling to* LISE, *boastfully*] Lise, look here! [*sniffing in the air exaggeratedly*] Oh, heavens! What a stench! [*going up to* CYRANO] You, Sir, must certainly have noticed how it smells in here! What is it?

CYRANO: [*slapping his face and sending him tumbling down*] A stinking bag of hot air!

[*The* CADETS *are all delighted to have found the old* CYRANO *again. They shout and leap around and turn somersaults.*]

ACT III

ROXANE'S KISS

A small square in the old Marais. The houses are old and the streets are narrow. On the right is ROXANE'S *house and the wall of her garden, which is overhung with thick foliage. There is a window and balcony over the door and a bench in front of the house. By the use of the bench and some stones jutting out of the wall, it is easy to climb to the balcony.*

Opposite ROXANE'S *house is an old house in the same style of brick and stone. The knocker on the door is bandaged with linen like a sore thumb.*

At the rising of the curtain, the DUENNA *is seated on the bench. The window on* ROXANE'S *balcony is wide open.* RAGUENEAU *is standing near the door dressed in a sort of livery. He has just finished relating something to the* DUENNA, *and is wiping his eyes.*

Scene i

RAGUENEAU, *the* DUENNA. *Then* ROXANE, CYRANO, *and two* PAGES.

RAGUENEAU: —and then off she went, with a musketeer! Deserted and financially ruined, I decided to put an end to it all, so I hanged myself. Just as my last breath was drawn, in comes Monsieur de Bergerac! He cuts me down, and gets me a job as his cousin's steward.

DUENNA: But how did you come to be ruined?

RAGUENEAU: Oh, Lise loved the warriors and I loved the poets! We gave away too much. Any cakes that were left by Apollo were quickly snapped up by Mars.† You can see why financial ruin didn't take very long.

DUENNA: [rising and calling up to the open window] Roxane, are you ready? They're waiting for us!

ROXANE'S VOICE: [from the window] I'm just putting on my cloak!

DUENNA: [to RAGUENEAU, showing him the door opposite] We're going over there to Clomire's house. She's receiving all the lady intellectuals and the poets today. They'll be reading a paper on "The Tender Passion."†

RAGUENEAU: "The Tender Passion"?

DUENNA: [in a mincing voice] Oh, yes! [calling up to the window] Roxane, if you don't come down quickly, we shall miss the talk on "The Tender Passion!"

ROXANE'S VOICE: I'm coming! I'm coming!

[There is the sound of stringed instruments approaching.]

CYRANO'S VOICE: [behind the scenes, singing] La la la la!

DUENNA: [surprised] Are they serenading us?

CYRANO: [followed by two pages with lutes] I tell you that's a demi-semi-qua-ver,† you demi-semi-fool!

FIRST PAGE: [ironically] You know, then, Sir, how to distinguish between semi-quavers and demi-semi-quavers?

CYRANO: Isn't every pupil of Gassendi† a musician?

PAGE: [playing and singing] La la!

CYRANO: [snatching the lute from him, and going on with the melody] In proof of which, I shall continue! La la la la!

ROXANE: [appearing on the balcony] Oh! It's you!

CYRANO: [singing his own words to the melody] I have come to serenade your lilies and pay my devotion to your roses!

ROXANE: I am coming down!

[She leaves the balcony.]

DUENNA: [pointing to the pages] How did you find these master musicians?

CYRANO: I won them in a bet with D'Assoucy. We were arguing forever over a question of grammar. Suddenly he points to these two louts whom he takes around with him as his escorts, and whom he thinks are great musicians. He says, "I will wager you a day's music!" And he lost! So, until the sun rises tomorrow, I'll have these lute-twangers at my heels, seeing all I

do, hearing all I say, and accompanying it all with melody. It was pleasant
at first, but I'm growing tired of it already. [*to the* MUSICIANS] Ho there! Go
serenade Montfleury for me! Play a dance for him! [*The pages go toward the
door.* CYRANO *speaks to the* DUENNA.] I have come, as I do every evening, to
ask Roxane whether— [*to the* PAGES, *who are going out*] Play a long time,
and play out of tune! [*to the* DUENNA] —whether her heart's desire is still
as faultless as he is handsome!

ROXANE: [*coming out of the house*] Ah! How handsome he is, and how brilliant in wit! Oh, how I love him!

CYRANO: [*smiling*] Christian has a brilliant wit?

ROXANE: Brighter than even your own, cousin!

CYRANO: I'm happy to hear it!

ROXANE: I would have thought it impossible that here could be a man on
this earth skilled enough to say so sweetly all the pretty nothings that
mean so much! At times it seems his mind is far away and his inspira-
tion is fading. But then, all of a sudden, he says such bewitching and
enchanting things to me!

CYRANO: [*incredulously*] No! It can't be true!

ROXANE: Why must you think that? Just like a man! Because he's handsome,
you assume he must be dull.

CYRANO: Does he speak well about love?

ROXANE: Not only does he *speak* superbly about it, but he *teaches* it!

CYRANO: And how does he write?

ROXANE: Even better! Listen to this! [*reciting*] "The more of my poor heart you
take, the larger my heart grows!" [*triumphantly to* CYRANO] How do you
like those lines?

CYRANO: Pooh!

ROXANE: It goes on: "And, since I must show some target for Cupid's cruel
dart, if you must keep mine, then give me your heart!"

CYRANO: Lord! First he has too much of a heart, then not enough! How
much heart does the fellow want?

ROXANE: Oh, you're being terrible! You're just jealous!

CYRANO: [*starting*] What do you mean?

ROXANE: It's your poet's jealousy! You envy that he writes so well! Listen
to this, and tell me if it's not the sweetest thing you've ever heard: "My
heart to yours gives but one cry: if kisses by letter could fly, then kisses
would soar, my love, straight from my fingertips and on to your lovely
lips, if kisses by letter could fly!"

CYRANO: [*smiling approvingly in spite of himself*] Well! Those last lines are—
[*correcting himself, and speaking disdainfully*] They are trite enough!

ROXANE: And listen to this—

CYRANO: [enchanted] Do you know all his letters by heart?

ROXANE: Every one of them!

CYRANO: How flattering that is!

ROXANE: They are the words of a master!

CYRANO: [modestly] Come, now—a master?

ROXANE: Yes, a master!

CYRANO: All right then. He's a master.

DUENNA: [coming down quickly] Here comes Monsieur de Guiche! [to CYRANO, pushing him toward the house] In with you! It's best he doesn't see you. It might put him on the scent—

ROXANE: [to CYRANO] The scent of my secret! He loves me, and he's powerful. If he finds out I'm in love with someone else, all is lost! He could ruin everything!

CYRANO: [entering the house] As you wish.

[DE GUICHE appears.]

Scene ii

ROXANE, DE GUICHE, the DUENNA standing a little way off.

ROXANE: [curtsying to DE GUICHE] I was just going out.

DE GUICHE: I've come to say goodbye.

ROXANE: Where are you going?

DE GUICHE: To the war.

ROXANE: Ah!

DE GUICHE: Yes, I leave tonight.

ROXANE: Oh!

DE GUICHE: We've gotten our orders. We're to lay siege to Arras.†

ROXANE: Ah, a siege?

DE GUICHE: It seems that my going away doesn't move you at all.

ROXANE: [politely] No, no...

DE GUICHE: I am heartbroken. Will I ever see you again? And if so, when? Have you heard that I've been named commander?

ROXANE: [indifferently] Bravo!

DE GUICHE: In the Guards regiment.

ROXANE: [startled] What! The Guards?

DE GUICHE: Yes, where your cousin serves, that swaggering boaster. I'll find a way to revenge myself on him at Arras.

ROXANE: [choking] The Guards are going to Arras?

DE GUICHE: [laughing] Yes, it's my regiment.

ROXANE: [*aside, while falling down onto the bench*] Christian!

DE GUICHE: What's the matter?

ROXANE: [*deeply moved*] Oh, I am in despair! To think that the man I love will be at war!

DE GUICHE: [*surprised and delighted*] You say such sweet words to me! It's the first time! And just when I must leave you!

ROXANE: [*changing her tone and fanning herself*] You say you're going to take revenge on my cousin?

DE GUICHE: Are you on his side?

ROXANE: Oh, no! I'm against him!

DE GUICHE: Do you see him often?

ROXANE: Very rarely.

DE GUICHE: He is seen all the time with one of the cadets…a young fellow named Newvillen…Neuviller…

ROXANE: Is he a tall gentleman?

DE GUICHE: Yes, and fair-haired.

ROXANE: Yes, reddish-blond hair!

DE GUICHE: Handsome.

ROXANE: Not very much.

DE GUICHE: But rather stupid.

ROXANE: One would think so, to look at him! [*changing her tone*] How are you planning to take your revenge on Cyrano? If you're thinking of putting him in the midst of all the shooting, then that plan won't work very well. You see, he loves danger. In the middle of all the terrible action is the place he would *want* to be. I know a far better way for you to wound his pride.

DE GUICHE: What is it? Tell me!

ROXANE: Leave him and his fellow cadets behind when the regiment marches to Arras! Let them spend the whole war powerless and idle! This is the thing that will enrage him! If you cheat Cyrano of his chance to engage in mortal danger, you will be punishing him severely!

DE GUICHE: [*coming nearer*] Oh, woman! Only a woman could devise such a subtle trick!

ROXANE: He'll eat his heart out! And his friends will gnaw angrily at their fingernails from being deprived of battle. See, this is the way you can avenge yourself.

DE GUICHE: Do you love me a little, then? [ROXANE *smiles.*] I would almost believe it proves your love, the way you're helping me with my cause.

ROXANE: It certainly is proof of love!

DE GUICHE: [*showing some sealed papers*] Here are the marching orders. They'll be sent instantly to each company, except…[*He takes one paper out.*] this one! It's the one for the Cadets. [*He puts it in his pocket.*] This one I will keep. [*laughing*] Ha! ha! ha! Cyrano! His love of battle! You really can play tricks on people! You, of all ladies!

ROXANE: Sometimes!

DE GUICHE: [*coming close to her*] Oh, how I love you! You drive me mad! Listen! I know that I'm supposed to leave tonight, but how can I leave now that I've learned your heart has been touched? Nearby, in the Rue d'Orleans, is a monastery founded by Father Athanasius, the syndic of the Capuchins.† While it's true that no laymen may enter, I think I can work it out with the good Fathers. Their sleeves are wide enough to hide me in. 'Tis they who serve Richelieu's private chapel, and out of respect for my uncle, they will do as I tell them. Everyone will think I have left Paris. And then I will come to you, masked. Let me have your permission to delay my departure just one day, sweet lady!

ROXANE: But if people find out, then your glory—

DE GUICHE: Bah!

ROXANE: But the siege at Arras—

DE GUICHE: It can begin without me. Please, grant me your permission.

ROXANE: No!

DE GUICHE: Please say yes!

ROXANE: [*tenderly*] It is my duty to forbid you.

DE GUICHE: Ah!

ROXANE: You must go! [*aside*] Christian stays here. [*aloud*] I want you to be heroic—Antoine!

DE GUICHE: Oh, heavenly word! You do love, then—

ROXANE: Yes, the one I tremble for.

DE GUICHE: [*ecstatic*] Ah! I shall go then! [*He kisses her hand.*] Are you content?

ROXANE: Yes, Antoine!

[*He goes out.*]

DUENNA: [*making a mocking curtsy behind his back*] Yes, Antoine!

ROXANE: [*to the* DUENNA] Do not speak a word of what I have done! Cyrano would never pardon me for stealing his fighting from him! [*She calls toward the house.*] Cousin!

Scene iii

ROXANE, *the* DUENNA, CYRANO.

ROXANE: We're going to Clomire's house. [*She points to the door opposite.*] Alcandre and Lysimon are to discourse!

DUENNA: [*putting her little finger in her ear*] Yes, but my little finger tells me we shall miss hearing them.

CYRANO: It would be a pity to miss those monkeys!

[*They have come to Clomire's door.*]

DUENNA: Oh, look! The knocker is wrapped with cloth! [*speaking to the knocker*] So they have gagged you, noisy one, lest you disturb the fine speakers!

[*She lifts if carefully and knocks with precaution.*]

ROXANE: [*seeing that the door is opening*] Let's go in! [*on the threshold, to* CYRANO] If Christian comes, as I feel sure he will, please tell him to wait for me!

CYRANO: [*quickly, as she is going in*] Listen! [*She turns.*] You always choose a subject to speak about with Christian. Tell me, which subject will you ask him to speak on tonight?

ROXANE: Oh—

CYRANO: [*eagerly*] Yes?

ROXANE: Do you promise you won't tell him?

CYRANO: I promise.

ROXANE: I shall not choose a subject at all. Instead, I will tell him to speak on whatever he wishes. I don't want him to prepare a speech. This time, I want him to speak his thoughts as they come. I'll tell him to speak to me of love, and to speak of it splendidly!

CYRANO: [*smiling*] Very good!

ROXANE: But secret!

CYRANO: Secret.

ROXANE: Not a word.

[*She enters and shuts the door.*]

CYRANO: [*when the door is shut, bowing to her*] A thousand thanks!

[*The door opens again, and* ROXANE *puts her head out.*]

ROXANE: If he knew what I just told you, he would prepare a speech in advance!

CYRANO: We wouldn't want that to happen!

BOTH TOGETHER: Shhhhh!

[*The door shuts.*]

CYRANO: [*calling*] Christian!

Scene iv

CYRANO, CHRISTIAN

CYRANO: I know what's needed for tonight. Here's your chance to truly impress her. Come, we cannot waste any time. Put away that sulky expression. Come to your house with me, and I'll teach you—

CHRISTIAN: No!

CYRANO: Why?

CHRISTIAN: I will wait for Roxane here.

CYRANO: What? Are you crazy? Come quickly with me and learn—

CHRISTIAN: No! No, I say! I'm tired of these borrowed letters and borrowed speeches! I'm tired of acting a part and fearing all the time. It helped me in the beginning, but now I know she loves me! I'm afraid no longer! From now on, I will speak for myself!

CYRANO: Good heavens!

CHRISTIAN: What makes you think I cannot speak at all? I'm not such a fool anymore. I've learned a lot from your lessons. I'll be able to speak without your help. You'll see! At least I know enough to take her in my arms! [*seeing* ROXANE *come out from Clomire's house*] It is she! Oh, Cyrano! Don't leave me!

CYRANO: [*bowing*] Speak for yourself, my friend, and take your chances.

[*He disappears behind the garden wall.*]

Scene v

CHRISTIAN, ROXANE, *the* DUENNA.

ROXANE: [*coming out of Clomire's house with a group of friends, bowing and saying goodbye to them*] Goodbye, Barthenoide! Alcandre! Gremione!

DUENNA: [*bitterly disappointed*] We missed the speech on "The Tender Passion."

[*She goes into* ROXANE'S *house.*]

ROXANE: [*still bowing to her friends*] Goodbye, Urimedonte! [*They all bow to* ROXANE *and to each other, and then separate, going up different streets.* ROXANE *suddenly sees* CHRISTIAN.] It's you! [*She goes to him.*] Night is falling and no one is around. Let's sit. Please speak, and I will listen.

CHRISTIAN: [*sits by her on the bench; there is a silence.*] Oh! I love you!

ROXANE: [*shutting her eyes*] Yes, speak to me of love.

CHRISTIAN: I love you!

ROXANE: Yes, that's the theme, but elaborate on it.

CHRISTIAN: I...

ROXANE: Go on, elaborate!

CHRISTIAN: I love you so!

ROXANE: Oh, without a doubt! But what else?

CHRISTIAN: And I would be—Oh!—I would be so glad—so glad—if you would love me! Oh, Roxane, tell me so!

ROXANE: [*with a little grimace*] I hoped for cream, but you're giving me water! Explain to me how you love me!

CHRISTIAN: Oh, utterly!

ROXANE: Come, come! Untangle those knotted thoughts!

CHRISTIAN: I'd love to kiss your throat!

ROXANE: Christian!

CHRISTIAN: I love you!

ROXANE: [*half-rising*] You've already said that!

CHRISTIAN: [*eagerly, trying to detain her*] No, no! I don't love you!

ROXANE: [*reseating herself*] Well, at least that's a change.

CHRISTIAN: I adore you!

ROXANE: [*rising and going further away*] Oh!

CHRISTIAN: Oh, I'm growing foolish!

ROXANE: [*dryly*] And that displeases me—almost as much as it would displease me if you grew ugly.

CHRISTIAN: But—

ROXANE: Find your eloquence that seems to have flown away!

CHRISTIAN: I...

ROXANE: Yes, you love me. I already know that. Good night!

[*She goes toward her house.*]

CHRISTIAN: Oh, don't go yet! I shall tell you—

ROXANE: [*opening the door*] That you adore me? I've heard that enough. Go away!

CHRISTIAN: But I—

[She shuts the door in his face.]

CYRANO: *[who has re-entered unseen]* Well, what a success that was!

Scene vi

CHRISTIAN, CYRANO, *two* PAGES.

CHRISTIAN: Help me!

CYRANO: Not I!

CHRISTIAN: But I shall die unless I win her respect back at once!

CYRANO: And how, in the devil's name, do you expect me to teach you right this moment—

CHRISTIAN: *[seizing his arm]* Oh, there she is!

[The window of the balcony is now lighted up.]

CYRANO: *[with great emotion]* Her window!

CHRISTIAN: Oh! I shall die!

CYRANO: Shhh! Speak softly!

CHRISTIAN: *[in a whisper]* I shall die!

CYRANO: It's dark now...

CHRISTIAN: So?

CYRANO: We can repair the damage—although I'm not sure you deserve it! Stand there, in front of the balcony! I'll hide beneath it and tell you what to say.

CHRISTIAN: But—

CYRANO: Hold your tongue!

PAGES: *[reappearing at the back, and shouting to* CYRANO*]* Ho there!

CYRANO: Hush!

[He signs to them to speak softly.]

FIRST PAGE: *[in a low voice]* We've played the serenade to Montfleury as you asked!

CYRANO: *[quickly, in a low voice]* Go! Hide over there! One at this street corner and one at that one! And if a passer-by should intrude, play a tune for him!

SECOND PAGE: What tune shall we play, oh great student of Gassendi?

CYRANO: If a woman comes, play something happy. If a man, something sad! *[The* PAGES *disappear, one at each street corner.* CYRANO *speaks to* CHRISTIAN*]* Call her!

CHRISTIAN: Roxane!

CYRANO: [*picking up stones and throwing them at the window*] Some pebbles! Wait a while!

ROXANE [*half-opening the window*] Who calls me?

CHRISTIAN: It is I!

ROXANE: Who's that?

CHRISTIAN: Christian!

ROXANE: [*disdainfully*] Oh, you?

CHRISTIAN: I want to speak with you.

CYRANO: [*under the balcony, to* Christian] Good. Speak soft and low.

ROXANE: No, you speak like a fool!

CHRISTIAN: Oh, have pity on me!

ROXANE: No! I don't think you love me anymore!

CHRISTIAN: [*prompted by* CYRANO] You think I no longer love you? Oh, great heaven, but I love you more and more!

ROXANE: [*who was about to shut the window, pausing*] That's a little better.

CHRISTIAN: [*prompted by* CYRANO] My love for you grows and grows. It batters me like a cruel and restless child using my heart for a cradle.

ROXANE: [*coming out onto the balcony*] That's better! But if you think that Cupid is so cruel, then you should have stifled this newborn love while it was still in its cradle!

CHRISTIAN: [*prompted again*] Oh, Madame, I tried. But this love was as strong as Hercules† from the moment it was born.

ROXANE: Still better!

CHRISTIAN: [*prompted again*] And this Hercules in my heart strangled the twin serpents of Pride and Doubt!

ROXANE: [*leaning over the balcony*] Well said! But why do you halt so much? Has your ability for imagination weakened?

CYRANO: [*drawing* CHRISTIAN *under the balcony, and slipping into his place*] Let me do it! This has become too critical!

ROXANE: Why do you speak so hesitantly tonight?

CYRANO: [*imitating* CHRISTIAN, *in a whisper*] It is so dark that my words must grope their way in the blackness to find your ear.

ROXANE: But *my* words don't have the same difficulty.

CYRANO: They find their way down to me at once? That's no surprise, then! It's because their home is in my heart, and my heart is so large that they cannot help but fall into the right place. Your ear, however, is small! And of course, your words come fast because they fall from such a height, while mine must climb up to you, and that takes time!

ROXANE: It seems that your last words have learned to climb.

CYRANO: They've become better at such exercise!

ROXANE: It is true that I seem to speak from high above you.

CYRANO: Yes, and so far above that a hard word from you would kill me if it were to fall on my heart.

ROXANE: [*moving*] I'm coming down.

CYRANO: [*hastily*] No!

ROXANE: [*showing him the bench under the balcony*] Then won't you stand on the bench so I can see you?

CYRANO: [*starting back, alarmed*] No!

ROXANE: Why not?

CYRANO: [*overcome with emotion*] Let us stay like this for a while. It's so sweet to have this rare occasion when our hearts can speak without our bodies seeing one another.

ROXANE: But why should we want to speak without seeing one another?

CYRANO: Oh, because it's so sweet! We are half-hidden and half-revealed. You see the dark folds of my cloak and I see the glimmering whiteness of your dress. I am but a shadow, and you are a bright shining light! Do you know what such a moment does to me? I may have been eloquent in the past but—

ROXANE: Oh, you *have* been!

CYRANO: Yet not until tonight has my speech sprung so directly from my heart!

ROXANE: Why not?

CYRANO: Up until now, I spoke uncertainly. I've been so intoxicated by your beauty. Your eyes radiate and make me dizzy. But tonight, I think I am able to find speech for the first time!

ROXANE: 'Tis true, your voice even sounds a little different.

CYRANO: [*coming nearer, passionately*] Yes, I speak with a new tone! In the sheltering dusk, I dare to be myself for once—at last! [*He stops, falters.*] What have I said? Please pardon me. It's all so enchanting, and so sweet and new!

ROXANE: New? How so?

CYRANO: [*deeply moved and trying to compose himself again*] It's a new feeling for me to at last speak sincerely. Up until now, my heart feared that it would be mocked—

ROXANE: But why?

CYRANO: Because of its mad passion! My heart has masked itself with witty words to hide itself from curious eyes. I've aimed to bring stars down from the sky, but, fearing ridicule, I've stooped to pick wild flowers instead!

ROXANE: Wild flowers are sweet!

CYRANO: Yes, but not tonight. Tonight I aim for the star!

ROXANE: Oh! You've never spoken quite like this before!

CYRANO: Tonight I want to leave behind all of Cupid's arrows and quivers. I don't want to speak about the trite little symbols of love—the sentimental kinds of things that all lovers already speak about. Instead, I want to speak in a fresh, pure language—one that comes directly from my heart. For why should we sip little thimblefuls of dull fashionable waters, when, instead, we can quench our souls' thirst by drinking from the great flooding river!

ROXANE: But what about your wit? Your elegant speeches?

CYRANO: If I have used my witty speech to gain your attention at the first, then it would be an outrage and an insult to this night, and to Nature herself, to speak such sugary, flowery words again. Just look up at the stars! The quiet sky will ease our hearts of all things artificial. If love is expressed in terms too refined, then the real feeling is lost. The truth of love itself becomes buried among all the flowery embellishments of poetic language.

ROXANE: But wit, and elegant language—

CYRANO: They are a crime when it comes to love! It is hateful to turn honest loving into a game! When the moment comes—and I pity those who never know that moment—and the real feeling of love exists in us, premeditated words are futile and only make the soul sad!

ROXANE: Well, if that moment has come for us, what words will you use now?

CYRANO: All words! Whatever words come to me, and even as they come, I'll fling them in a wild cluster and not wrap them in a careful bouquet. I love you! I am mad! I am suffocating with love for you! Your name rings in my heart like a bell. When I think of you, I tremble, and the bell shakes and rings out your name! Everything you do I love! I remember every action of yours that I ever witnessed! I know that last year on the twelfth of May, you changed the way you wore your hair. I am so used to taking your hair for daylight itself that, just as one stares at the sun and sees a red blot on all things, when I turn away after looking at you, I see a radiant image imprinted on everything!

ROXANE: [*in a trembling voice*] Yes, this is love.

CYRANO: Yes, the feeling which fills me is true love! Fierce and jealous and sad, yet never selfish. I would gladly lay down my own happiness for yours, even if you were never to know it. And even if I end up far away from you and lonely, I will be content just to hear a happy echo of the joy I once brought you! Each glance from you makes me virtuous and brave in new and unknown ways. Do you begin to understand me? Now, after all this time, have you begun to understand? Do you feel my soul climbing up to you through the darkness of this night? Oh, it is too sweet, too incredible, that I should speak this way and that you should listen! Even in moments when my hopes rose so high, I never could have hoped for this much! I could die peacefully right now. My words have had the power to make you tremble! You *are* trembling, I can feel it! I can feel the quivering of your hand echoing down through the jasmine branches!

[*He passionately kisses one of the hanging branches.*]

ROXANE: Oh, I am trembling and weeping! I am yours! You have conquered all of me!

CYRANO: Then let death come! It is I who have conquered you! There is just one thing I dare ask you—

CHRISTIAN: [*under the balcony*] A kiss!

ROXANE: [*drawing back*] What?

CYRANO: Oh!

ROXANE: Did you ask—

CYRANO: I— [*to* CHRISTIAN, *whispering*] Fool! You're moving too fast!

CHRISTIAN: She is in such a loving mood that I must take advantage of the moment!

CYRANO: [*to* ROXANE] Yes, I asked for a kiss, but I spoke thoughtlessly. Shame on me!

ROXANE: [*disappointed*] You withdraw your request so quickly!

CYRANO: Yes, I withdraw, but without really withdrawing! I'm afraid I have offended your modesty. If so, please do not grant me that kiss!

CHRISTIAN: [*to* CYRANO, *pulling him by his cloak*] Why?

CYRANO: Silence, Christian! Hush!

ROXANE: [*leaning over*] What are you whispering?

CYRANO: I'm chiding myself for my overly bold advances. I say to myself, "Silence, Christian!" [*The lutes begin to play.*] Hark! Wait a minute! I hear footsteps! [ROXANE *shuts the window.* CYRANO *listens to the lutes, one of which plays a merry tune and the other a melancholy tune.*] How strange. They play both a sad tune and a happy one. What does it mean? Neither man nor woman? Aha! It's a monk!

[*Enter a capuchin* FRIAR, *with a lantern. He goes from house to house, looking at every door.*]

Scene vii

CYRANO, CHRISTIAN, *a capuchin* FRIAR.

CYRANO: [*to the* FRIAR] Hello there, new Diogenes.† What are you searching
   for this time?
FRIAR: I'm looking for the house of Madame—
CHRISTIAN: Oh, make him go away!
FRIAR: Madeleine Robin—
CHRISTIAN: What could he want?
CYRANO: [*pointing to a street at the back*] It's that way! Straight ahead!
FRIAR: I thank you, and will pray my rosary for you.

[*He goes out.*]

CYRANO: Good luck and blessings to you!

[*He goes back to* CHRISTIAN.]

Scene viii

CYRANO, CHRISTIAN.

CHRISTIAN: Win for me that kiss!
CYRANO: No!
CHRISTIAN: Sooner or later…
CYRANO: 'Tis true! Sooner or later the moment will come when your mouths
   are sure to meet. Thanks to your fair mustache and her rose petal lips!
   [*to himself*] I'd rather it should come thanks to—

[*There is a sound of shutters reopening.* CHRISTIAN *goes in again under the
balcony.*]

Scene ix

CYRANO, CHRISTIAN, ROXANE.

ROXANE: [*coming out onto the balcony*] Are you still there? We were speaking
   of a—
CYRANO: A kiss! The word is sweet! Do not let your lips shrink from it! If the

word burns your sweet mouth, what would the kiss itself do? Oh, don't let it frighten you or make you shy. You've already left playful banter behind and glided easily from smile to sigh, and then from sigh to weeping. Glide gently further still. It is only a heartbeat from tear to kiss!

ROXANE: Hush, hush!

CYRANO: When all is said and done, what is a kiss? It's simply an oath made more certain, a sealed promise, the heart's confirmation of a pact. It's a secret whispered to the mouth instead of the ear, a stolen moment that makes time eternal, a communion perfumed like the spring's wild flowers. A kiss allows for one to live through the beating of another's heart, and to taste the very soul of another on one's lips!

ROXANE: Hush, hush!

CYRANO: A kiss, Madame, is honorable. Even the Queen of France granted a kiss to her favorite lord!

ROXANE: But what has that got to do with us?

CYRANO: [speaking more warmly] I have suffered in silence just as Buckingham did. He adored a queen,† just as I do. He was sad but faithful, and so am I.

ROXANE: And you are as handsome as Buckingham!

CYRANO: [aside, suddenly cool] Oh, yes. I forgot!

ROXANE: Please climb up here and pick me as your flower.

CYRANO: [pushing CHRISTIAN toward the balcony] Climb!

ROXANE: Communion perfumed like spring's wild flowers...!

CYRANO: Climb!

CHRISTIAN: [hesitating] But somehow it doesn't feel quite right anymore.

ROXANE: A stolen moment...!

CYRANO: [still pushing CHRISTIAN] Go, blockhead, climb!

[CHRISTIAN springs forward, and by way of the bench, the branches, and the pillars, climbs up to the balcony.]

CHRISTIAN: Ah, Roxane!

[He takes her in his arms, and bends over her lips.]

CYRANO: Oh, what a strange pain in my heart! The kiss is so near! I am like Lazarus at the feast.† But still a crumb or two falls down to me from the rich man's plate. Because it is my heart that receives you, Roxane. For, as you press your lips against his, it is my words that you kiss! [The lutes play.] What now? Both a sad song and a happy song again? It must be the monk! [He begins to run as if he came from a long way off, and then cries out towards ROXANE's house.] Hello!

ROXANE: What is it?

CYRANO: I—I was just passing by. Is Christian here?

CHRISTIAN: [*astonished*] Cyrano!

ROXANE: Hello, cousin!

CYRANO: Good evening, cousin!

ROXANE: I'm coming down!

[*She disappears into the house. The* FRIAR *reenters at the back.*]

Scene x

CYRANO, CHRISTIAN, ROXANE, *the* FRIAR, RAGUENEAU.

FRIAR: 'Tis here, I'm sure of it—Madame Madeleine Robin.

CYRANO: But you asked for Rolin before!

FRIAR: No, I didn't! I asked you for the house of Madame Robin—R-O-B-I-N!

ROXANE: [*appearing on the threshold, followed by* RAGUENEAU, *who carries a lantern, and* CHRISTIAN] What is it?

FRIAR: A letter.

CHRISTIAN: A letter?

FRIAR: [*to* ROXANE] It must be about some holy business! It's from a wealthy lord!

ROXANE: [*to* CHRISTIAN] De Guiche!

CHRISTIAN: How dare he!

ROXANE: Oh, he won't be able to bother me forever! It is you whom I love! [*unsealing the letter and reading in a low voice with the aid of* RAGUENEAU'S *lantern*] "Lady, the drums beat and my regiment prepares to leave, but I secretly stay behind. I have dared to disobey your order. I am here in a monastery. I will come to you tonight. This letter comes to you by way of a poor fool of a monk who knows not what he carries. Your lips have smiled on me too sweetly. I cannot go until I've seen them once again! Please send all your servants away tonight so we may meet in private. I hope you will pardon my boldness. I remain, always, your—" Etcetera, etcetera. [*to the* MONK] Father, you must hear what this letter says. [*Everyone gathers around her and she reads out loud.*] "Lady, the Cardinal has spoken, and his wish is law, no matter how much you may disagree with it. I have sent you this letter by way of a discreet and intelligent holy man. It is the will of the Cardinal that, in your own house, this very night [*She turns the page.*] this monk shall perform the holy rite of matrimony. Unknown to all the world, Christian shall become your husband. I know that he is not your first choice, and that you rather dislike him, but you must obey the Cardinal in this matter. Rest assured that you will be rewarded in heaven for your sacrifice in this matter. I remain your humble and faithful—" Etcetera.

FRIAR: [*with great delight*] Oh, I knew it could only be holy business, coming from such a noble lord!

ROXANE: [*to* CHRISTIAN, *in a low voice*] I'm very good at reading letters, aren't I?

CHRISTIAN: Hmm!

ROXANE: [*aloud, with despair*] But this is horrible!

FRIAR: [*who has turned his lantern on* CYRANO] Are you the one she is to marry?

CHRISTIAN: No, I am!

FRIAR: [*turning the light on* CHRISTIAN, *and startled by his handsome face*] But...

ROXANE: [*quickly*] Oh, I must have overlooked the postscript. It says, "Give twenty pistoles† to the monastery."

FRIAR: Oh! Most worthy lord! [*to* ROXANE] Do you resign yourself to this marriage?

ROXANE: [*with the look of a* MARTYR] I resign myself! [*While* RAGUENEAU *opens the door, and* CHRISTIAN *invites the* FRIAR *to enter, she whispers to* CYRANO.] Oh, keep de Guiche occupied! He will be here soon! Don't let him enter until—

CYRANO: I understand! [*to the* FRIAR] How much time will you need to perform the marriage ceremony?

FRIAR: About a quarter of an hour.

CYRANO: [*pushing them all toward the house*] Go! I'll stay out here.

ROXANE: [*to* CHRISTIAN] Come!

[*They enter.*]

CYRANO: How can I stall de Guiche for so long? [*He jumps onto the bench and climbs up to the balcony.*] Up I go! I've got a plan! [*The lutes begin to play a sad tune.*] What's that? [*The tune grows more intense.*] It must be a man approaching this time! [*He stands on the balcony, pulls his hat over his eyes, takes off his sword, wraps himself in his cloak, and then leans over.*] It's not too high. [*He strides across the balcony, and pulls toward him a long branch of one of the trees that are by the garden wall. He then hangs onto the branch with both hands, ready to let himself fall.*] I shall disturb this peaceful atmosphere!

Scene xi

CYRANO, DE GUICHE.

DE GUICHE: [*entering, with mask on, feeling his way in the dark*] What can that cursed friar be doing?

CYRANO: Damn! What if he recognizes my voice! [*Letting go with one hand, he pretends to turn an invisible key.*] There! I've unlocked my native Bergerac accent!

DE GUICHE: [*looking at the house*] I cannot see well at all through this mask! [*He is about to enter, when* CYRANO *leaps from the balcony, holding onto the branch, which bends, dropping him between the door and* DE GUICHE. *He then pretends to fall heavily, as if from a great height, and lies flat on the ground, motionless, as if stunned.* DE GUICHE *jumps back, startled.*] What's this? [*When he looks up, the branch has sprung back into its place. He sees only the sky, and is lost in amazement.*] Where did this man fall from?

CYRANO: [*sitting up and speaking with a thick Gascon accent*] From the moon!

DE GUICHE: From the moon?

CYRANO: [*in a dreamy voice*] What time is it?

DE GUICHE: He's lost his mind, for sure!

CYRANO: What time is it? What country is this? What month? What day?

DE GUICHE: But—

CYRANO: I'm still dazed and confused from the fall!

DE GUICHE: Sir!

CYRANO: I just fell like a bomb, straight from the moon!

DE GUICHE: [*impatiently*] Oh, come on!

CYRANO: [*rising, in a fierce voice*] I fell from the moon, I tell you!

DE GUICHE: [*stepping back*] Yes, fine, so be it. [*aside*] He's raving mad!

CYRANO: [*walking up to him*] I say from the moon! And I don't mean it metaphorically!

DE GUICHE: But—

CYRANO: Was it a hundred years ago or just a minute ago? I cannot guess how much time has passed since I was on that yellow sphere up there!

DE GUICHE: [*shrugging his shoulders*] Fine, then. Just let me pass.

CYRANO: [*stepping in his way*] Where am I? Tell me the truth! Don't spare me! Where have I just fallen like a shooting star?

DE GUICHE: Oh, good Lord!

CYRANO: The fall was lightning quick! I had no time to choose where I might land! Oh, tell me where the weight of my posterior has landed me! Am I on earth or another moon?

DE GUICHE: I tell you, Sir—

CYRANO: [*with a screech of terror, which makes* DE GUICHE *jump back*] No! Can it be? I've landed on a planet where men have black faces!

DE GUICHE: [*putting a hand to his face*] What?

CYRANO: [*pretending to be greatly alarmed*] Am I in Africa? Are you a native?

DE GUICHE: [*who has remembered his mask*] Oh, my mask—

CYRANO: [*pretending to be somewhat reassured*] Ah, then I must be in Venice!† Or Rome?

DE GUICHE: [*trying to pass*] A lady waits for me.

CYRANO: Ah! Then I must be in Paris!

DE GUICHE: [*smiling in spite of himself*] This fool is quite comical!

CYRANO: You're smiling?

DE GUICHE: Yes, I'm smiling, but I would still like to get by!

CYRANO: [*beaming with joy*] I've landed back in Paris! [*acting completely at ease now; laughing, dusting himself off, bowing*] Oh, please pardon me! I'm all soaked with cloud-water! My eyes are still full of stardust and I have planet fur on my shoes! [*picking something off his sleeve*] And a comet's hair stuck on my jacket! [*He puffs as if to blow it away.*]

DE GUICHE: [*completely exasperated*] Sir!

CYRANO: [*Just as* DE GUICHE *is about to pass, he holds out his leg as if to show him something and stops him.*] Look! See the tooth mark in my leg from where the Great Bear† bit me! And when I veered to avoid Neptune's† trident, I fell right into the Scales!† My weight is still registered on those scales, up there in heaven! [*hurriedly preventing* de Guiche *from passing, and detaining him by the button of his jacket*] I swear to you that if you squeezed my nose, it would spout milk!

DE GUICHE: Milk?

CYRANO: From the Milky Way!

DE GUICHE: Oh, go to hell!

CYRANO: [*crossing his arms*] Sir, I just fell from heaven! Would you believe me if I told you that Sirius† wears a nightcap? It's true! [*confidentially*] The other Bear† is still too small to bite! [*laughing*] I went straight through the Lyre† and snapped a cord! [*proudly*] Some day I shall write the whole thing in a book!† The small gold stars that have stuck to my cloak will serve as asterisks on the printed page!

DE GUICHE: Enough of this! Let me—

CYRANO: Oh, you're a sly one!

DE GUICHE: Sir!

CYRANO: You're trying to worm it all out of me! You want me to tell you what the moon is made of, and whether or not anyone lives there! I know what you're up to!

DE GUICHE: [*angrily*] No, no! I just want—

CYRANO: To know how I got up there? It was by a method all my own!

DE GUICHE: [*growing tired*] He's mad!

CYRANO: [*contemptuously*] I didn't copy Regiomontanus'† eagle! Nor did I make a version of Archytas'† pigeon! Neither of those! I tell you I got there by my own invention!

DE GUICHE: Indeed, he's a fool, but an educated fool!

CYRANO: No, I'm not an imitator of other men! [DE GUICHE *has succeeded in getting by, and goes toward* ROXANE'S *door.* CYRANO *follows him, ready to stop him by force.*] Six new methods, all invented by my own brain!

DE GUICHE: [*turning around*] Six?

CYRANO: [*quickly and fluently*] First, I lay my naked body on the ground and dab myself all over with drops of water. Then I let the sun's fierce rays suck me up just as they suck up the morning dew!

DE GUICHE: [*surprised, making one step toward* CYRANO] Ah! That makes one!

CYRANO: [*stepping back, and enticing him further away*] Second, I surround a chest with twenty mirrors. The mirrors focus the sun's rays directly upon the chest, heating up the air inside it. The air becomes rarefied and the chest rises up like a balloon, with myself inside it!

DE GUICHE: [*making another step*] That makes two!

CYRANO: [*still stepping backward*] Or, with my mechanical skills, I build a giant grasshopper out of steel. I use gunpowder to propel it, and with each leap, it launches me upward to the skies!

DE GUICHE: [*unconsciously following him and counting on his fingers*] Three!

CYRANO: Or, since smoke rises, I fill a giant globe with smoke. The globe rises, and carries me away!

DE GUICHE: [*still following Cyrano, and becoming more and more astonished*] Well, that makes four!

CYRANO: Or, since the goddess of the moon likes to hunt cattle, I coat my body with cattle marrow and get drawn up by her bow and arrow!

DE GUICHE: [*amazed*] Five!

CYRANO: [*who, while speaking, has drawn* DE GUICHE *to the other side of the square near a bench*] Or, I sit upon an iron platform and throw a magnet into the air. It's a very smart method! The magnet will pull up the iron platform with me on it. Then, I simply throw the magnet up again and it pulls the platform up further! And on and on, until I reach the moon!

DE GUICHE: Those are six excellent methods! Which one of them did you choose?

CYRANO: Why, none of them! I chose a seventh!

DE GUICHE: Astonishing! What was it?

CYRANO: Try to guess.

DE GUICHE: This madman has becoming quite interesting!

CYRANO: [making a noise like that of ocean waves, and gesturing strangely] Hoo! Hoo!

DE GUICHE: What does that mean? .

CYRANO: Can't you guess?

DE GUICHE: Certainly not!

CYRANO: The tide! When the moon was full, I soaked myself in the sea and laid myself down by the shore. In the same way that it pulls the ocean up and causes the tides, the moon pulled *me* up! I was pulled straight up by my head, since that part of me held the most moisture, due to my wet and matted hair! I was gently rising, just like an angel in flight, when all of a sudden I felt a shock! And then—

DE GUICHE: [overcome by curiosity, sitting down on the bench] And then what?

CYRANO: Oh! And then—[suddenly returning to his natural voice] The quarter hour is up. I'll detain you no more. The marriage vows have been exchanged.

DE GUICHE: [springing up] What? Am I mad? That voice! [The door of the house opens. LACKEYS appear carrying lighted candelabra. The stage lighting becomes brighter. CYRANO gracefully takes off his hat, which he had kept pulled down in order to hide his face.] That nose! Cyrano?

CYRANO: [bowing] At your service. They've just been married.

DE GUICHE: Who? [He turns around. Behind the lackeys appear ROXANE and CHRISTIAN, holding hands. The FRIAR follows them, smiling. RAGUENEAU also holds a candlestick. The DUENNA follows at the rear, bewildered and wearing a dressing gown.] Good Lord!

Scene xii

The same, with ROXANE, CHRISTIAN, the FRIAR, RAGUENEAU, the LACKEYS, the DUENNA.

DE GUICHE: [to ROXANE] You? [recognizing CHRISTIAN, in amazement] And he? [bowing, with admiration, to ROXANE] How clever and cunning your little trick! [to CYRANO] My compliments to you as well, master inventor! Your story would stop even the angels on their way into heaven!

Be sure to write all the details down. It certainly would make a great book!

CYRANO: [*bowing*] I will take your advice.

FRIAR: [*showing with satisfaction the two lovers to* DE GUICHE] A handsome couple, brought together by you, Sir!

DE GUICHE: [*with an icy look*] Yes. [*to* ROXANE] Say goodbye to your husband, Madame.

ROXANE: Why?

DE GUICHE: [*to* CHRISTIAN] The regiment is departing. Join it!

ROXANE: The regiment is going off to battle?

DE GUICHE: Without doubt.

ROXANE: But the cadets aren't going, are they?

DE GUICHE: Oh, yes, they're going! [*drawing out the paper he had put in his pocket*] Here's the order. [*to* CHRISTIAN] Baron, take it and deliver it at once!

ROXANE: [*throwing herself into* CHRISTIAN'S *arms*] Christian!

DE GUICHE: [*sneeringly to* CYRANO] The wedding night is a long way off, I think!

CYRANO: [*aside*] He thinks that bothers me!

CHRISTIAN: [*to* ROXANE] Oh, let me kiss you once more!

CYRANO: Come, come, that's enough!

CHRISTIAN: [*still kissing* ROXANE] You don't know how hard it is to leave her!

CYRANO: [*trying to draw him away*] I do know.

[*There is the sound of drums beating a march in the distance.*]

DE GUICHE: The regiment starts!

ROXANE: [*to* CYRANO, *holding back* CHRISTIAN, *whom* CYRANO *is drawing away*] I trust you to protect him! Promise me that nothing shall put his life in danger!

CYRANO: I will do my best, but I cannot promise anything.

ROXANE: But swear to me that you'll make sure he is careful!

CYRANO: Again, I'll do my best, but—

ROXANE: Promise me he won't suffer from the cold during the siege!

CYRANO: I'll do everything I can—

ROXANE: Promise me that he'll be faithful!

CYRANO: I'm sure he will be, but—

ROXANE: Promise to make him write to me often!

CYRANO: [*pausing*] That is something I can promise!

Curtain.

ACT IV

THE CADETS OF GASCONY

A post occupied by the company of CARBON DE CASTEL-JALOUX *at the siege of Arras. In the background is an embankment across the whole stage. Beyond is a view of plains extending to the horizon. The countryside is covered with entrenchments. The walls of Arras and the outlines of its roofs can be seen in the distance. Tents, weapons, armor, and drums are strewn about. Day is breaking with a faint glimmer of yellow sunrise in the east. Sentinels keep watch at various points. Campfires are burning. The cadets of Gascony, wrapped in their cloaks, are sleeping.* CARBON DE CASTEL-JALOUX *and* LE BRET *are keeping watch. They are very pale and thin.* CHRISTIAN *sleeps among the others in his cloak in the foreground, his face illuminated by the fire. There is silence.*

Scene i

CHRISTIAN, CARBON DE CASTEL-JALOUX, LE BRET, *the* CADETS, *then* CYRANO.

LE BRET: It's terrible!
CARBON: Not a morsel of food left.
LE BRET: Mordious!
CARBON: [*making a sign that he should speak lower*] Curse under your breath. You will awaken them. [*to the* CADETS] Hush! Go back to sleep. [*to* LE BRET] He who sleeps can dine by dreaming of food.

89

LE BRET: That's not much comfort to those who cannot sleep! What starvation!

[*Firing is heard in the distance.*]

CARBON: Oh, damn their firing! It will wake my boys. [*to the* CADETS, *who lift up their heads*] Go back to sleep!

[*Firing is heard again, nearer this time.*]

A CADET: [*moving*] Damn! Again!
CARBON: 'Tis nothing! It's just Cyrano coming back!

[*Those who have lifted up their heads prepare to sleep again.*]

A SENTINEL: [*from offstage*] Halt! Who goes there?
VOICE OF CYRANO: Bergerac.
SENTINEL: [*on the embankment*] Stop! Who goes there?
CYRANO: [*appearing at the top of the embankment*] It's Bergerac, you idiot!

[*He comes down.* LE BRET *advances anxiously to meet him.*]

LE BRET: Heavens!
CYRANO: [*making signs that he should not awaken the others*] Hush!
LE BRET: Are you wounded?
CYRANO: No. You should know by now they make a habit of missing me every morning.
LE BRET: This is too much! To risk your life every morning in order to deliver letters!
CYRANO: [*stopping before* CHRISTIAN]
    I promised that he would write often. [*He looks at* CHRISTIAN.] He sleeps. How pale he is! But still handsome, despite his sufferings. If his poor lady-love knew that he is dying of hunger...
LE BRET: Get yourself to bed, quickly.
CYRANO: Don't scold me, Le Bret! The risk I take is smaller than you think. I've found an easy spot to pass through the Spanish lines, where the men go to sleep drunk every night.
LE BRET: You should try to bring us back some food next time.
CYRANO: A man must carry no weight if he is to get by there! But there will be a surprise for us tonight. If I'm not mistaken, the French will either eat or die tonight.

LE BRET: Oh! What's going on? Tell me!

CYRANO: No, not yet. I'm not certain of it yet. You'll see.

CARBON: We're the besiegers, and yet we're starving! How disgraceful!

LE BRET: Alas, this siege is full of complications! While we're besieging, we ourselves are caught in a trap and are besieged by the Cardinal Infante of Spain.†

CYRANO: It would come full circle if he were besieged as well!

LE BRET: This isn't funny. I'm serious.

CYRANO: Oh! Of course!

LE BRET: To think that you should risk your precious life everyday, for the sake of a letter. [*seeing him turning to enter the tent*] Where are you going?

CYRANO: To write another one!

[*He enters the tent and disappears.*]

Scene ii

The same, with all but CYRANO. *The day is breaking in a rosy light. The town of Arras is golden on the horizon. The report of cannon fire is heard in the distance, followed immediately by the beating of drums far away to the left. Other drums are heard much nearer. There are sounds of stirring in the camp and voices of officers in the distance.*

CARBON: [*sighing*] The reveille! [*The* CADETS *move and stretch themselves.*] Nourishing sleep is at an end! I know what their first cry will be!

A CADET: [*sitting up*] I'm so hungry!

ANOTHER: Oh, I'm dying of hunger!

TOGETHER: Oh!

CARBON: Up with you!

THIRD CADET: I cannot move a limb!

FOURTH CADET: Nor can I!

FIRST: [*looking at himself in a piece of armor*] My tongue is yellow. The air we've been living on is not quite in season—it's hard on the digestion.

ANOTHER: I'd give my coronet for a bit of cheese!

ANOTHER: If I don't get something for the juices in my stomach to work on, I'll give up and retire to my tent like old Achilles!†

ANOTHER: Oh, something, anything! Even just a crust!

CARBON: [*going to the tent and calling softly*] Cyrano!

ALL THE CADETS: We're dying!

CARBON: [*continuing to speak under his breath at the opening of the tent*] Help me, Cyrano. You always know what to say to make them feel better. Come, cheer them up.

SECOND CADET: [*rushing toward another who is munching on something*] What are you eating there?

FIRST CADET: Cannon wadding fried in axle-grease! It's poor game-hunting around here!

A CADET: [*entering*] I've been hunting game!

ANOTHER: [*following him*] And I've been after fish!

ALL: [*rushing to the two newcomers*] Well!—What have you brought?—A pheasant?—A carp?—Come, show us quick!

FISHER: A minnow.

HUNTER: One tiny sparrow.

ALL TOGETHER: [*exasperated*] It's more than we can bear! We'll mutiny!

CARBON: Cyrano! Come to my aid!

[*The daylight has now come.*]

Scene iii

The same, with CYRANO.

CYRANO: [*appearing from the tent, very calm, with a pen stuck behind his ear and a book in his hand*] What's wrong? [*There is silence. He speaks to the* FIRST CADET.] Why do you drag yourself around so sadly?

CADET: I have something in my feet which weighs them down.

CYRANO: And what might that be?

CADET: My stomach!

CYRANO: I have the same problem!

CADET: But aren't you bothered by it?

CYRANO: No, being so thin only makes us look taller!

A THIRD: My stomach's hollow.

CYRANO: Then it shall make a fine drum to bang during the assault!

ANOTHER: I have a ringing in my ears.

CYRANO: No, no! That can't be! A hungry stomach has no ears!

ANOTHER: Oh, for a morsel of anything, with just a dab of oil!

CYRANO: [*pulling off the* CADET'S *helmet and holding it out to him*] Here's your salad!

ANOTHER: What, in God's name, can we eat?

CYRANO: [*throwing him the book which he is carrying*] The Iliad!† A little food for thought!

ANOTHER: The prime minister in Paris[†] gets *his* four meals a day!

CYRANO: It would be courteous of him to send you a few partridges!

SAME CADET: Yes, it would! And wine too!

CYRANO: A little Burgundy, please, Cardinal!

ANOTHER: I'm as ravenous as a giant!

CYRANO: Then feast on some of your giant's fat!

FIRST CADET: [*shrugging*] You're always so quick with your pointed words!

CYRANO: Yes, pointed words! And I hope that when I die, I shall die making a pointed word for a good cause. I'll die a soldier's death by a soldier's sword, wielded by some brave adversary. I'll die on blood-stained ground, not in a sickbed, with a pointed word on my lips, and a *real* point within my heart.

ALL THE CADETS: I'm hungry!

CYRANO: All you think about is food! Bertrandou the fifer, you were a shepherd once. Draw your fife from its leather case and play for these greedy, gluttonous soldiers. Play some sweet country songs to remind us of our Gascon homes. Play those songs that softly echo the dear voices of family, in which each note calls to us like a little sister. Play those tunes that rise slowly, like the smoke-wreaths rise from the hearthstones of our native villages. Their music strikes the air like Gascon patois! [*BERTRANDOU seats himself, and gets his flute ready.*] Your flute is sadly at war now, but it was not always a warrior. As your fingers dance upon its stem in a bird-like minuet, remember that flutes were not always made of wood, but were made first out of simple reeds. Use your flute to recall those pastoral days, the soul-time of your youth, in country pastures! [*The old man begins to play a Gascon tune.*] Listen to the music, Gascons! It's no longer the piercing fife of battle, but beneath his fingers, the flute of the woods! No more the call to combat, it's now the love-song of the wandering goat-herds! Listen! It's the valley, the wetlands, the forest, the sunburnt shepherd boy with scarlet beret, the dusk of evening on the Dordogne River![†] 'Tis Gascony! Listen, Gascons, to the music!

[*The CADETS sit with bowed heads. Their eyes have a far-off look as if they are dreaming. Once in a while, they furtively wipe away their tears with their cuffs and the corner of their cloaks.*]

CARBON: [*to CYRANO in a whisper*] But you're making them weep!

CYRANO: Yes, but for homesickness. It's a nobler pain than hunger. It's a pain of the soul, not the body. I'm pleased to see their pain changed. Heartache is better than stomach-ache.

CARBON: But aren't you weakening their courage by playing with their hearts?

CYRANO: [*making a sign to a drummer to approach*] Not at all! The hero that
sleeps inside of every Gascon is easily awakened. All it takes is—

[*He makes a signal and the drum begins to beat.*]

ALL THE CADETS: [*standing up and rushing to take up their weapons*] What?
What is it?
CYRANO: [*smiling*] See! One roll of the drum is enough! Goodbye dreams,
regrets, native land, love! All that the pipe brought forth, the drum has
chased away!
A CADET: [*looking toward the back of the stage*] Ugh! Here comes Monsieur
de Guiche.

[*All the* CADETS *mutter irritably.*]

CYRANO: [*smiling*] That's a flattering welcome!
A CADET: We are sick to death of him!
ANOTHER: With his lace collar over his armor, acting like he's a fine
gentleman!
ANOTHER: A soldier should not wear linen over steel!
THE FIRST: Unless he's using it to bandage a boil on his neck!
THE SECOND: He's not a true soldier! He's a scheming courtier!
ANOTHER: He's his uncle's nephew!
CARBON: But he's still a Gascon.
THE FIRST: Oh, but a false Gascon! I don't trust him at all. True Gascons
are madmen, but he is too sane. There's nothing more dangerous than
a rational Gascon!
LE BRET: He's so pale!
ANOTHER: Oh, he's hungry, just as we are. But since he wears gilded studs
on his armor, *his* stomach-ache glitters in the sunlight!
CYRANO: [*hurriedly*] Let's not look like we're suffering! Take out your cards
and pipes and dice! [*They all begin lighting pipes and spreading out games
on the drums, the stools, the ground, and on their cloaks.*] And I shall read
Descartes.[†]

[*He walks up and down, reading a little book which he has drawn from his
pocket.* DE GUICHE *enters. Everyone appears absorbed and happy.* DE GUICHE *is
very pale. He goes up to* CARBON.]

Scene iv

The same, with DE GUICHE.

DE GUICHE: [*to* CARBON] Good day! [*They examine each other. De Guiche speaks in an aside, with satisfaction.*] He's quite green!

CARBON: [*looking at* DE GUICHE *with the same sort of satisfaction and also speaking in an aside*] His cheeks are sunken and his eyes are as big as saucers!

DE GUICHE: [*looking at the* CADETS] So! Here are the rebels! I've been hearing from all sides that you country louts scoff at me—your colonel! It seems that you mountain-bred aristocrats harbor a disdain for me, calling me a plotter and a scheming courtier! I hear that it doesn't please your mightiness to see a lace collar on my armor! You're all simply enraged by the fact that a man can be still be a Gascon without looking like a ragged beggar! [*There is silence. Everyone continues to smoke and to play.*] Shall I command your captain to punish you? No.

CARBON: Let me remind you that these are my men, and I would refuse to punish them.

DE GUICHE: Ah!

CARBON: These men are of *my* company. I take orders only from headquarters.

DE GUICHE: Is that so? Fine, then. [*addressing himself to the cadets*] I am above your taunts, because it's well known how I've shown myself in this war. Just yesterday, at Bapaume,† I beat back the Count of Bucquoi.† I assembled my men and we charged on him three separate times!

CYRANO: [*without lifting his eyes from his book*] Yes, and don't forget the part about your white scarf.

DE GUICHE: [*surprised and gratified*] Oh, you've heard that detail? It's true! I'll tell you how it happened. While turning about to recall the troops for the third charge, I was swept up with a band of fugitives. They bore me with them, and we came dangerously close to the enemy. I was in peril of capture or sudden death! I quickly had the idea to loosen the scarf which told my military rank and I let it fall. This way, I was unnoticed and was able to leave the swarm. I went back, rallied my men, and we charged and scattered them! What do you say to that, Sir?

[*The* CADETS *pretend not to be listening, but the cards and the dice-boxes remain suspended in their hands, the smoke of their pipes in their cheeks. They wait.*]

CYRANO: I say that Henry the Fourth would never have stripped himself of his scarf,† no matter the danger.

[*There is silent delight among the cadets. The cards fall, the dice rattle, the smoke is puffed.*]

DE GUICHE: But it was a good trick! And it worked!

[*The* CADETS *again suspend their movements and wait.*]

CYRANO: Oh, that may be true! But I don't believe in lightly abdicating the honor of being the enemy's target. [*Cards and dice fall again, and the cadets smoke with delight.*] We have very different ideas of what courage is, Sir. If I had been there when your scarf fell, I would have picked it up and put it on myself.

DE GUICHE: Oh, that's just Gascon bragging!

CYRANO: Bragging? Give the scarf to me. I promise that tonight I will lead the assault while wearing it across my chest.

DE GUICHE: Another Gascon boast! You know very well that my scarf now lies on the river bank in enemy territory. The place is riddled with gunfire! No one can bring it back!

CYRANO: [*drawing the scarf from his pocket, and holding it out to him*] Here it is.

[*There is silence. The cadets stifle their laughter in their cards and dice-boxes.* DE GUICHE *turns and looks at them. They instantly become serious and return to their games. One of them whistles indifferently the tune that was just played by the fifer.*]

DE GUICHE: [*taking the scarf*] I thank you. And now I shall make a signal that I was unable to make until now.

[*He goes to the embankment and waves the scarf three times.*]

ALL: What's he doing?

SENTINEL: [*from the top of the embankment*]
I see a man running away down there!

DE GUICHE: [*descending*] He's a false Spanish spy. He's extremely useful to me. I give him false news to carry to the enemy, and such news influences their decisions!

CYRANO: He's a traitor and a scoundrel!

DE GUICHE: [*carelessly knotting his scarf*] But he's extremely helpful to us. Now, what were we talking about? Ah! I have news for you. Last night, the Marshal secretly left for Dourlens in order to bring back food and drink for us. But to ensure that he would be able to return to camp more easily, he took most of the troops with him. If we get attacked now, we'll be in serious trouble. Half of the army is absent from the camp!

CARBON: Yes, if the Spaniards knew this, it would be terrible for us. But they know nothing?

DE GUICHE: Oh, they know. And they will attack us.

CARBON: Ah!

DE GUICHE: My false spy came to warn me of their attack. He told me, "I can have them attack at whichever point you'd like them to, by telling them that it's the point which is least defended. Where do you want it to happen?" I answered, "Leave the camp and watch for my signal. I will sign to you from the point I have chosen."

CARBON: [*to the* CADETS] Make ready!

[*All the* CADETS *rise. There are sounds of swords being picked up and belts being buckled.*]

DE GUICHE: It will happen in one hour.

FIRST CADET: Oh, in that case...

[*They all sit down again and take up their games.*]

DE GUICHE: [*to* CARBON] The Marshal will be on his way back, so we must keep the enemy occupied here for as long as we can.

CARBON: How do you propose we do that?

DE GUICHE: By letting them continue their attack until every last one of your cadets are killed.

CYRANO: Ah! So this is your revenge!

DE GUICHE: I am not saying that if I loved you all, I would have chosen differently. As boastful and courageous as you are, you are my best choice. In this way, I serve both my King and my grudge at the same time.

CYRANO: Permit me to express my gratitude.

DE GUICHE: I know you love to fight against the odds. I hope you're not complaining now.

[*He goes up with* CARBON.]

CYRANO: [*to the* CADETS] We shall add to the Gascon coat of arms a new mark! Among its six bars of blue and gold, we'll add one more—a blood-red bar that was missing before!

[DE GUICHE *speaks in a low voice with* CARBON *at the back. Orders are given. Preparations go forward.* CYRANO *goes up to* CHRISTIAN, *who stands with crossed arms.*]

CYRANO: [*putting his hand on* CHRISTIAN'S *shoulder*] Christian?

CHRISTIAN: [*shaking his head*] Roxane!

CYRANO: Yes, I know.

CHRISTIAN: If I could only, at the very least, say goodbye to her in a letter!

CYRANO: I had a suspicion that today might be the day, so I already wrote—
    [*He draws a letter out of his jacket.*]

CHRISTIAN: Show it to me!

CYRANO: Shall I—

CHRISTIAN: [*taking the letter*] Yes! [*He opens it and reads.*] Wait a minute!

CYRANO: What?

CHRISTIAN: This little spot!

CYRANO: [*taking the letter, with an innocent look*] A spot?

CHRISTIAN: It's a tear!

CYRANO: Alas, poets are so good at inventing emotion that they sometimes
    get caught up in it themselves! This letter was so sad and moving that
    I wept myself while writing it!

CHRISTIAN: You wept? But why?

CYRANO: Oh, death itself is nothing. But to never see her again! That is
    something worse than death! To think that I shall never— [CHRISTIAN
    looks at him.] I mean, to think that we shall—[*quickly*] I mean, that
    you—

CHRISTIAN: [*snatching the letter from him*] Give me that letter!

[*A distant rumbling is heard far off in the camp.*]

VOICE OF SENTINEL: Who goes there?

[*Shots and voices and carriage bell are heard.*]

CARBON: What is it?

SENTINEL: [*on the embankment*] 'Tis a carriage!

[*Everyone rushes to see.*]

CRIES: A carriage? In the camp? It's coming! The enemy! Fire on it! No! The
    coachman! What did he say? "On the King's service!"

[*Everyone is on the embankment, staring. The bells come nearer.*]

DE GUICHE: The King's service? How?

[*Everyone comes down and falls into line.*]

CARBON: Hats off, everyone!

DE GUICHE: The King's service! Get in line, all of you! Don't you know how to welcome a king?

[The carriage enters at full speed covered with dust and mud. The curtains are drawn closed. Two LACKEYS *follow behind. The carriage stops suddenly.]*

CARBON: Beat the salute!

[A roll of drums sounds. The CADETS *take off their hats.]*

ROXANE: *[jumping down from the carriage]* Good day!

[All are bowing to the ground, but at the sound of a woman's voice every head is instantly raised.]

Scene v

The same, with ROXANE.

DE GUICHE: On the King's service! You?

ROXANE: Yes, I come in the service of the king called love! What other king is there?

CYRANO: Great God!

CHRISTIAN: *[rushing forward]* Why have you come?

ROXANE: This siege is going on too long!

CHRISTIAN: But—

ROXANE: I will tell you all!

CYRANO: *[who, at the sound of her voice, has stood still, rooted to the ground, afraid to raise his eyes]* My God! I don't dare to look at her!

DE GUICHE: You cannot stay here!

ROXANE: *[merrily]* Yes, I can! Who will give me a drum to sit on? *[She seats herself on the drum that is rolled forward.]* Thank you! *[She laughs.]* My carriage was fired at! *[proudly]* It looks just like a pumpkin, doesn't it? And my footmen like rats turned into handsome men, just like in the fairy tale! *[blowing a kiss to* CHRISTIAN] Good morning! *[examining them all]* You don't look very cheerful! Don't you know it's a long way from Paris to Arras? *[seeing* CYRANO] Cousin! I'm delighted to see you!

CYRANO: *[coming up to her]* But how, in Heaven's name—?

ROXANE: How did I find my way here? It was simple enough. I just had to keep going until I saw the countryside laid to waste. Ah, what horrors were there! If I had not seen it, I would never have believed it! Well, gentlemen, if this is the way you serve your king, I would certainly rather serve mine!

CYRANO: But this is sheer madness! Where in the devil's name did you get through?

ROXANE: Where? Through the Spanish lines, of course!

FIRST CADET: Only a woman could get away with something like that!

DE GUICHE: But how did you pass through their lines?

LE BRET: Yes, that must have been extremely difficult!

ROXANE: Not really. I simply drove calmly forward in my carriage, and whenever some proud Spaniard stopped me, I gave him my sweetest smile. And since Spaniards are the most gallant gentlemen in the world—after Frenchmen, of course—they allowed me to pass on!

CARBON: True, that smile of yours makes a pretty passport! But were you not asked to give an account of where you were going, Madame?

ROXANE: Yes, frequently. And in answer, I would say, "I'm going to see my lover." At that word, the fiercest Spaniard of them all would gravely shut the carriage door, and, with a gesture that a king might envy, would signal to his men to lower the guns leveled at me. Then, with sad and graceful dignity, he would doff his hat and bow low to me, saying, "Pass on, Señorita!"

CHRISTIAN: But, Roxane—

ROXANE: Forgive me for saying "my lover." But think of it! If I had said "my husband" not one of them would have let me pass!

CHRISTIAN: But...

ROXANE: What's the matter?

DE GUICHE: You must leave here!

ROXANE: Must I?

CYRANO: Yes, and right now!

LE BRET: At once!

CHRISTIAN: Indeed, you must.

ROXANE: But why must I?

CHRISTIAN: [embarrassed] Because—

CYRANO: [also embarrassed] In three quarters of an hour—

DE GUICHE: [with the same look] Or less—

CARBON: [the same] It would be best if—

LE BRET: [the same] You might want to—

ROXANE: You're going to fight, aren't you? I'm staying here!

ALL: No, no!

ROXANE: He is my husband! [She throws herself into CHRISTIAN's arms.] They shall kill us both together!

CHRISTIAN: What a fiery look in your eyes!

ROXANE: You know what it signifies!

DE GUICHE: [*in despair*] This is a post of mortal danger!

ROXANE: [*turning around*] Mortal danger?

CYRANO: He should know. He stationed us here.

ROXANE: [*to* DE GUICHE] So! You wanted to make a widow out of me!

DE GUICHE: No! I swear to you—

ROXANE: I will not go! I'm reckless now, and I shall not move from here! Besides, it's quite amusing!

CYRANO: Oh! So the lady intellectual is now a heroine as well!

ROXANE: I am your cousin, Monsieur de Bergerac.

A CADET: We'll defend you well!

ROXANE: [*more and more excited*] I do not doubt that at all, my friends!

ANOTHER: [*ecstatically*] Ah! The whole camp smells like irises!

ROXANE: And what luck! I'm wearing a hat that will look so nice on the battlefield! [*looking at* DE GUICHE] Shouldn't you be going? Surely they'll begin the attack any moment!

DE GUICHE: I won't stand for this! I'm going to inspect the cannons. When I return, I hope to see that you've changed your mind!

ROXANE: Never!

[DE GUICHE *goes out.*]

Scene vi

The same, with all except DE GUICHE.

CHRISTIAN: [*begging*] Roxane!

ROXANE: No!

FIRST CADET: [*to the others*] She stays!

ALL: [*hurrying, hustling each other, tidying themselves for her*] A comb! Some soap! My uniform is torn! A needle! A ribbon! Lend me your mirror! Your mustache curler! A razor!

ROXANE: [*to* CYRANO, *who still pleads with her*] No! Nothing shall make me move from this spot!

CARBON: [*who, like the others, has been buckling, dusting, brushing his hat, settling his plume, and drawing on his cuffs, advances to* ROXANE, *and speaks ceremoniously.*] Since that is the case, let me present to you some of these gentlemen who are about to have the honor of dying before your eyes. [ROXANE *bows, and stands leaning on* CHRISTIAN'S *arm, while* CARBON *introduces the cadets to her.*] Baron de Peyrescous de Colignac!

THE CADET: [*bowing*] Madame.

CARBON: [*continuing*] Baron de Casterac de Cahuzac...Vidame de Malgouyre Estressac Lesbas d'Escarabiot...Chevalier d'Antignac-Juzet...Baron Hillot de Blagnac-Salechan de Castel Crabioules...

ROXANE: But how many names do you each have?

BARON HILLOT: Oh, too many to count!

CARBON: [*to* ROXANE] Please, open the hand which holds your handkerchief.

ROXANE: [*opens her hand, the handkerchief falls*] Why?

[*The whole company starts forward to pick it up.*]

CARBON: [*quickly raising it*] My company had no flag! But now they will have the most beautiful flag in all the camp!

ROXANE: [*smiling*] 'Tis a little small.

CARBON: [*tying the handkerchief on the staff of his lance*] But it's made of lace!

A CADET: [*to the rest*] I could die happy, having seen such a sweet face, if only I had something in my stomach!

CARBON: [*indignantly*] Shame on you! How can you speak of eating when such a lovely woman—

ROXANE: I'm starving too! It must be the brisk air. I'd like some pâté, some cold chicken and some good wine. Would you please bring it to me?

[*Everyone is confused and dismayed.*]

A CADET: You want all of that?

ANOTHER: But where on the earth shall we find it?

ROXANE: [*quietly*] In my carriage.

ALL: What!

ROXANE: All we must do is unpack it and serve it! Look a little closer at my coachman, gentlemen, and you'll recognize a most valuable man! All the sauces can be served hot, if you like!

THE CADETS: [*rushing to the carriage*] It's Ragueneau! [*loud cheers*] Oh! Bravo!

ROXANE: [*looking after them*] Poor fellows!

CYRANO: [*kissing her hand*] Kind fairy!

RAGUENEAU: [*standing on the seat of the carriage and proclaiming*] Gentlemen!

[*The* CADETS *cheer enthusiastically.*]

RAGUENEAU: The Spaniards, feasting their eyes on such a beautiful lady, failed to notice the beautiful feast that she was hiding!

[*The* CADETS *applaud.*]

CYRANO: [*in a whisper to* CHRISTIAN] Listen, Christian!
RAGUENEAU: They were so occupied with gallantry that they overlooked…
[*He draws a plate from under the seat, and holds it up.*] the galantine!

[*The* CADETS *applaud more. The dish passes from hand to hand.*]

CYRANO: [*still whispering to* CHRISTIAN] Please, let me have one word with you!
RAGUENEAU: They were so hypnotized by Beauty that they failed to notice…
[*He holds up a roasted pig on a platter.*] the Beast!

[*Enthusiastic cries ensue. All the* CADETS *reach out to the platter.*]

CYRANO: [*in a low whisper to* CHRISTIAN] I must speak to you!
ROXANE: [*to the* CADETS, *who come down with their arms laden with food*] Put it all on the ground!

[*She lays it all out on the grass, aided by the two lackeys who followed behind the carriage.*]

ROXANE: [*to* CHRISTIAN, *just as* CYRANO *is drawing him away*] Come and make yourself useful!

[CHRISTIAN *comes to help her.* CYRANO'S *uneasiness increases.*]

RAGUENEAU: Peacock with truffles!
FIRST CADET: [*radiant, coming down with a big slice of ham*] Thank God! We don't have to die without having had a gullet-full—[*quickly correcting himself on seeing* ROXANE] Pardon me! A civilized banquet, I mean!
RAGUENEAU: [*throwing down the carriage cushions*] The cushions are stuffed with quail!

[*The* CADETS *tear open the cushions, laughing and shouting.*]

THIRD CADET: Thank the Lord!
RAGUENEAU: [*throwing bottles of red and white wine down to the* CADETS] Flasks of rubies and flasks of topaz!

ROXANE: [*throwing a folded tablecloth at* CYRANO'S *head*] Unfold that napkin! Come, make it quick now!

RAGUENEAU: [*waving a lantern*] Each of the carriage-lamps is a little pantry of its own!

CYRANO: [*in a low voice to* CHRISTIAN, *as they arrange the cloth together*] I must speak with you before you speak to her.

RAGUENEAU: The handle of my whip is a sausage!

ROXANE: [*pouring out wine and helping with the food*] Since we're about to die, let's eat all this food ourselves. All for the Gascons! And, listen! If de Guiche comes back, we shall not invite him to our feast! [*going from one to the other*] There, there! You have time enough! Don't eat too fast. Here, have some wine. Why are you weeping?

FIRST CADET: It's all so good!

ROXANE: [*playing the part of the hostess, speaking quickly to all of them in turn*]Hush! Red or white? Some bread for Monsieur de Carbon! A knife, please! Pass your plate! A little of the crust? Some more? Let me help you! Some champagne? A wing?

CYRANO: [*who follows her, his arms laden with dishes, helping her to wait on everybody*] How I worship her!

ROXANE: [*going up to* CHRISTIAN] What would you like?

CHRISTIAN: Nothing.

ROXANE: Oh, you must! At least take this biscuit, soaked in wine!

CHRISTIAN: [*trying to detain her*] Oh! Tell me why you came here!

ROXANE: Wait! My first duty is to these poor men. Hush! In a few minutes—

LE BRET: [*who had gone up to pass a loaf of bread on the end of a lance to the sentry on the embankment*] De Guiche is coming!

CYRANO: Quick! Hide the bottles, plates, pie-dishes and meats! Everything! Hurry! Look as if nothing has been going on! [*to* RAGUENEAU] Get up on your seat! Is everything covered up?

[*In an instant everything has been pushed into the tents or hidden in jackets, cloaks and hats.* DE GUICHE *enters hurriedly and suddenly stops, sniffing the air. There is silence.*]

Scene vii

DE GUICHE: Something smells good here.

A CADET: [*singing casually*] La, la, la...

DE GUICHE: [*looking at him*] What's the matter with you? Your cheeks are flushed.

CADET: Nothing's the matter! It's just my blood boiling at the thought of the coming battle!

ANOTHER: Poom, poom-poom...

DE GUICHE: [*turning around*] What's that?

CADET: [*slightly drunk*] Oh, nothing! Just a little song!

DE GUICHE: Well, aren't you in a merry mood!

CADET: It's just that the approach of danger is intoxicating!

DE GUICHE: [*calling* CARBON DE CASTEL-JALOUX, *to give him an order*] Captain! I— [*He stops short on seeing him.*] By God! You too! How strangely happy you look!

CARBON: [*red in the face, hiding a bottle behind his back with an evasive movement*] Oh! I...

DE GUICHE: Listen. I have one cannon left, and I've carried it over there. [*He points.*] Your men can use it in case they need it.

A CADET: [*reeling slightly*] What a thoughtful action!

ANOTHER: [*with a gracious smile*] How sweet of you to think of us!

DE GUICHE: Good Lord! Have they all gone crazy? [*curtly*] Since you're not used to cannons, beware of the recoil on this one.

FIRST CADET: Pooh!

DE GUICHE: [*furious, going up to him*] Look here, you—!

CADET: Gascon cannons never recoil!

DE GUICHE: [*taking him by the arm and shaking him*] You're drunk! But with what?

CADET: [*loftily*] The smell of gunpowder!

DE GUICHE: [*shrugging his shoulders and pushing him away, then going quickly to* ROXANE] Quickly, Madame, have you made your decision?

ROXANE: Yes, I'm staying here.

DE GUICHE: No, you must go!

ROXANE: No! I'm staying.

DE GUICHE: If this is the way it's going to be, someone give me a musket.

CARBON: Why?

DE GUICHE: Because I, too, am staying.

CYRANO: At last! This is true bravery, Sir!

FIRST CADET: Then you *are* a Gascon after all, despite your lace collar!

ROXANE: What's all this about?

DE GUICHE: I will never leave any woman in danger.

SECOND CADET: [*to the first*] Listen! Don't you think we ought to give him something to eat?

[*All the food and drink reappears as if by magic.*]

DE GUICHE: [*eyes sparkling*] Food!

THIRD CADET: Yes, you'll see it appear from under every hat and coat!

DE GUICHE: [controlling himself, proudly] Do you think I'll eat your leftovers?

CYRANO: [saluting him] You're making progress.

DE GUICHE: [proudly, with a light touch of Gascon accent] I will fight without breaking my fast!

FIRST CADET: [with wild delight] Spoken like a true Gascon!

DE GUICHE: [laughing] I am a Gascon!

CADET: He's one of us!

[The CADETS shout and dance in delight.]

CARBON: [who had disappeared behind the embankment, reappearing on the ridge] I've lined up my pikemen. They're prepared to fight until the end.

[He points to a row of pikes, the tops of which are seen over the ridge.]

DE GUICHE: [bowing to ROXANE] Will you accept my hand, and accompany me while I inspect them?

[She takes it and they go up toward the embankment. All the CADETS take off their hats and follow them.]

CHRISTIAN: [going over to CYRANO] Tell me quickly!

[As ROXANE appears on the ridge, the tops of the lances disappear, lowered for the salute, and a shout is raised. She bows.]

PIKEMEN: [from outside] Hurrah!

CHRISTIAN: What is this secret?

CYRANO: If Roxane should—

CHRISTIAN: Should what?

CYRANO: If she should speak of the letters—

CHRISTIAN: Yes, go on!

CYRANO: Don't spoil it all by seeming surprised—

CHRISTIAN: Surprised at what?

CYRANO: I must explain to you! It's quite a simple matter. I was reminded of it just today upon seeing her. You've written—

CHRISTIAN: Tell me quickly!

CYRANO: You've written to her more often than you think.

CHRISTIAN: How so?

CYRANO: I took it upon myself to express your passion for you! At times I wrote to her without telling you!

CHRISTIAN: Ah, I see.

CYRANO: It's quite simple! No great matter!

CHRISTIAN: But we've been blockaded. How did you get the letters across?

CYRANO: Oh! I was able to get through before dawn.

CHRISTIAN: [*folding his arms*] And was *that* a simple matter too? Tell me, how often have "I" written? Twice a week? Three times? Four?

CYRANO: More often still.

CHRISTIAN: What! Every day?

CYRANO: Yes. Every day, twice a day.

CHRISTIAN: [*violently*] And you became so caught up in the mad joy of it that you risked your life—

CYRANO: [*seeing* ROXANE *returning*] Hush! Not in front of her!

[*He goes hurriedly into his tent.*]

Scene viii

ROXANE, CHRISTIAN. *In the distance cadets are coming and going.* CARBON *and* DE GUICHE *give orders.*

ROXANE: [*running up to* CHRISTIAN] Ah, Christian! At last!

CHRISTIAN: [*taking her hands*] Now, Roxane, tell me why you traveled such perilous roads and dealt with such vulgar soldiers in order to come here.

ROXANE: Your letters brought me here, my love!

CHRISTIAN: What do you mean?

ROXANE: It's your fault that I ran such risks! Your letters intoxicated me so much I lost my reason! So many letters! And each one better than the one before!

CHRISTIAN: Do you mean to say you came all this way just because of a few simple love letters?

ROXANE: Yes! You have no idea of the power those letters hold! Ever since that night under my window, when, in a voice all new to me, you bared your soul—ever since then I've adored you! And now, with all the letters of the past month, I hear your tender and true voice so close to me! So it *is* your fault, I say! It was your voice that drew me here. Penelope never would have stayed home and contented herself with her embroidering if her Ulysses could have written such letters! Instead, she would have cast everything aside and fled to join him, as mad for love as was Helen![†]

CHRISTIAN: But—

ROXANE: I read them over and over. I grew weak with love. I was entirely yours. Each separate page was like a flower petal, plucked from your soul, and sent wafting into mine. Imprinted in each burning word was a love so sincere, so powerful—

CHRISTIAN: A love sincere! And you really could feel that, Roxane?

ROXANE: Yes, I felt it!

CHRISTIAN: And so you have come...

ROXANE: Oh, Christian, my true love! Yes, I have come to you! If I were to throw myself down on my knees, I know you would lift me up. Therefore, I lay my soul down at your feet, and it cannot be raised. I've come to beg your forgiveness. And it seems a good time to ask for forgiveness, now that death is so near. I ask you to forgive me for the insult I did to you when I first loved you only for your handsome face!

CHRISTIAN: [horror-stricken] Roxane!

ROXANE: And later, when I grew less frivolous, I began to love you not just for your beauty, but also for your soul. I loved you for both of these things at once!

CHRISTIAN: And now?

ROXANE: Ah! And now, your true self has triumphed over your appearance! I now love you only for your soul!

CHRISTIAN: [stepping backward] Oh, Roxane!

ROXANE: But be happy. It must be torture for any noble soul to be loved only for beauty. For beauty is a poor disguise that is soon worn threadbare by time. Your dear thoughts have outshined the handsome face that won me in the beginning. And now I see clearer. Now I no longer see your beauty at all!

CHRISTIAN: Oh!

ROXANE: Do you still doubt your victory?

CHRISTIAN: [pained] Oh, Roxane!

ROXANE: I know. You cannot believe in such a love yet.

CHRISTIAN: I don't ask for such a love as that! All I want is for you to love me more simply!

ROXANE: Like so many other women have loved you? For shame! Let me show you a better kind of love!

CHRISTIAN: No! The first one was better!

ROXANE: Oh, how wrong you are! The way I love you now is the best kind of love! I love you for your true self. If you were less handsome—

CHRISTIAN: Hush!

ROXANE: I would love you still! Yes, even if you became ugly—[†]

CHRISTIAN: No! Don't say it!

ROXANE: Yes, I *will* say it!

CHRISTIAN: Even if I were ugly?

ROXANE: Yes, even so, I swear I'd love you still!

CHRISTIAN: My God!

ROXANE: Are you content at last?

CHRISTIAN: [*in a choked voice*] Yes.

ROXANE: What's wrong?

CHRISTIAN: [*gently pushing her away*] Nothing. I just need to have a word with someone. Just one moment.

ROXANE: But...

CHRISTIAN: [*pointing to the* CADETS] Those poor fellows are being deprived of you while you're here with me. Go on and speak to them and smile at them before they die.

ROXANE: [*deeply moved*] Dear Christian!

[*She goes up to the* CADETS, *who respectfully crowd around her.*]

Scene ix

CHRISTIAN, CYRANO. *At the back of the stage,* ROXANE *is speaking to* CARBON *and some* CADETS.

CHRISTIAN: [*calling toward* CYRANO'S *tent*] Cyrano!

CYRANO: [*reappearing, fully armed*] What's the matter? Why are you so pale?

CHRISTIAN: She does not love me!

CYRANO: What?

CHRISTIAN: It is you she loves!

CYRANO: No!

CHRISTIAN: She loves me only for my soul!

CYRANO: Truly?

CHRISTIAN: Yes! And that soul is you! Therefore it's you she loves—and you love her!

CYRANO: I?

CHRISTIAN: It's true! I know it!

CYRANO: Yes, it's true.

CHRISTIAN: You love her madly!

CYRANO: Yes, and even more than that!

CHRISTIAN: Then tell her so!

CYRANO: No!

CHRISTIAN: Why not?

CYRANO: Look at my face! You'll find your answer there!

CHRISTIAN: She told me she would love me even if I were ugly.

CYRANO: She said that?

CHRISTIAN: Yes! In those words!

CYRANO: I'm glad she told you that, but those are only words. Believe them if you want to, but I wouldn't. Take my word for it: never grow ugly. She'd be upset with me then!

CHRISTIAN: We'll see about that.

CYRANO: No! I'm begging you!

CHRISTIAN: Yes! Let her choose between us! Tell her everything!

CYRANO: No, no! I will not have it! Spare me this torment!

CHRISTIAN: Do you really believe that just because my face is handsome by chance, that *your* chance of happiness should be destroyed? That would be too unjust!

CYRANO: But do *you* think that just because I happen to have the gift of eloquence, I should let it kill *your* chance of happiness?

CHRISTIAN: Tell her everything!

CYRANO: You must not tempt me this way!

CHRISTIAN: I'm tired of being my own rival! I'll put an end to it!

CYRANO: Christian! Enough!

CHRISTIAN: Our marriage was made in secret. It can be easily dissolved if we survive.

CYRANO: My God! You still persist!

CHRISTIAN: I want to be loved for myself or not at all! I'm going over to the other side of the camp. While I'm gone, you must speak to her. Let her choose between the two of us!

CYRANO: It will be you.

CHRISTIAN: I pray that it will! [*He calls out.*] Roxane!

CYRANO: No! No!

ROXANE: [*coming up quickly*] Yes?

CHRISTIAN: Cyrano has something important to tell you.

[*She rushes over to* CYRANO. CHRISTIAN *goes out.*]

Scene x

Roxane, Cyrano. *Then* Le Bret, Carbon de Castel-Jaloux, *the* cadets, Ragueneau, de Guiche, *etc.*

Roxane: What is this urgent news?

Cyrano: [*in despair*] He's gone! [*to* Roxane] Oh, it's nothing! You know how he sees such importance in the most trivial things!

Roxane: [*warmly*] Did he doubt what I said? Ah, yes, I can tell—he doubted.

Cyrano: [*taking her hand*] But did you really speak the truth to him?

Roxane: Yes, I would love him even if he were...

[*She hesitates.*]

Cyrano: Does it embarrass you to say that word in front of me?

Roxane: I...

Cyrano: [*smiling sadly*] It won't hurt me! Say it! You'd love him if he were ugly!

Roxane: Yes!

[*A shot is heard outside, but* Cyrano *keeps talking.*]

Cyrano: [*passionately*] Even if he were hideous?

Roxane: Hideous! Yes!

Cyrano: Disfigured?

Roxane: Yes!

Cyrano: Grotesque?

Roxane: He could never be grotesque to me!

Cyrano: You'd love him the same way?

Roxane: Yes! No—even more!

Cyrano: [*losing command over himself, speaking in an aside*] My God! It's true! Maybe love really is within my reach! [*to* Roxane] I...Roxane... listen—

Le Bret: [*entering hurriedly*] Cyrano!

Cyrano: [*turning around*] What?

Le Bret: Hush!

[*He whispers something to him.*]

Cyrano: [*letting go of* Roxane's *hand and exclaiming*] Oh, God!

Roxane: What is it?

Cyrano: [*to himself, stunned*] It's all over now.

[*More shots are heard.*]

ROXANE: What's the matter? Listen! Another shot!

[*She goes up to look outside.*]

CYRANO: It's too late! Now I can never tell!
ROXANE: [*trying to rush out*] What's happened?
CYRANO: [*rushing to stop her*] Nothing!

[*Some* CADETS *enter, trying to hide something they are carrying. They huddle close around it, preventing* ROXANE *from seeing what it is.*]

ROXANE: Those men... [CYRANO *tries to draw her away.*] You were about to
     tell me something...
CYRANO: Tell you something? Oh, it was nothing, I swear! [*solemnly*] I
     swear that Christian's soul, his nature, was...[*quickly correcting himself*]
     is the noblest and the greatest—
ROXANE: Was? [*with a loud scream*] Oh!

[*She rushes up, pushing everyone aside.*]

CYRANO: It's all over now!
ROXANE: [*seeing* CHRISTIAN *lying on the ground, wrapped in his cloak.*] Oh,
     Christian!
LE BRET: [*to* CYRANO] Struck by the first shot of the enemy!

[ROXANE *flings herself down by* CHRISTIAN. *Sounds of gunfire, clashing of arms, and beating of drums are heard outside.*]

CARBON: [*with sword in the air*] We're being attacked! Get your muskets!

[*He rushes over the embankment, followed by the* CADETS.]

ROXANE: Christian!
VOICE OF CARBON: [*from the other side*] Quick! Prepare yourselves!
ROXANE: Christian!
CARBON: Fall in line!
ROXANE: Christian!
CARBON: Ready your matches!†
[RAGUENEAU *rushes up, bringing water in a helmet.*]

CHRISTIAN: [*in a dying voice*] Roxane!

[ROXANE *tears a piece of her dress and dips it into the water. She then presses it against* CHRISTIAN'S *wound, trying to stop the bleeding.* CYRANO *whispers quickly into* CHRISTIAN'S *ear while she is distracted.*]

CYRANO: I told her everything. She still loves you.

[CHRISTIAN *closes his eyes.*]

ROXANE: Yes, my love?
CARBON: Draw your ramrods!
ROXANE: [*to* CYRANO] He's not dead, is he?
CARBON: Open your charges with your teeth!
ROXANE: His cheek is growing cold against my own!
CARBON: Ready! Aim!
ROXANE: [*seeing a letter in* CHRISTIAN'S *jacket*] A letter! It's for me!

[*She opens it.*]

CYRANO: [*aside*] My letter!
CARBON: Fire!

[*Musket shots ring out, along with shouts and noises of battle.*]

CYRANO: [*trying to disengage his hand, which* ROXANE *is holding on her knees*] But Roxane, the battle is raging!
ROXANE: [*detaining him*] Please stay with me for a while. He's dead. You were the only one who really knew him. [*weeping quietly*] He was a wondrous and beautiful man, wasn't he?
CYRANO: [*standing up, with his hat off*] Yes, Roxane.
ROXANE: An inspired poet.
CYRANO: Yes, Roxane.
ROXANE: With a pure and brilliant mind.
CYRANO: Yes.
ROXANE: A heart too deep for shallow minds to comprehend; a spirit both subtle and charming.
CYRANO: [*firmly*] Yes, Roxane.
ROXANE: [*flinging herself on the dead body*] He is dead!
CYRANO: [*aside, while drawing his sword*] Yes, and let me die today as well. For, unknowing, it is I that she mourns, over his body.

[*Trumpets sound in the distance.*]

DE GUICHE: [*appearing on the embankment, bareheaded, with a wound on his forehead, in a thunderous voice*]
  That's the signal! The French are bringing provisions into camp! Hold out a little longer!

ROXANE: There is blood on the letter, and tears!

A VOICE: [*from outside, shouting*] Surrender!

VOICE OF CADETS: No!

RAGUENEAU: [*standing on the top of his carriage, watching the battle over the edge of the embankment*] The danger is at its greatest!

CYRANO: [*to DE GUICHE, pointing to ROXANE*] I will join the charge! You take her away!

ROXANE: [*kissing the letter, in a faint and choked voice*] Oh, God! His tears! His blood!

RAGUENEAU: [*jumping down from the carriage and rushing toward her*] She's fainted!

DE GUICHE: [*on the embankment, to the cadets, with fury*] Stand fast!

A VOICE: [*outside*] Lay down your arms!

CADETS: No!

CYRANO: [*to DE GUICHE*] You've proved your valor, Sir. [*pointing to ROXANE*] Now, hurry out of here and save her!

DE GUICHE: [*rushing to ROXANE, and carrying her away in his arms*] I will do so! If you can hold out, victory will be ours!

CYRANO: Good. [*calling out to ROXANE, whom DE GUICHE and RAGUENEAU are carrying away in a fainting condition*] Farewell, Roxane!

[*There is a great tumult, with shouts and screams from all sides. CADETS reappear, wounded and falling. CYRANO, rushing to the battle, is stopped by CARBON DE CASTEL-JALOUX, who is streaming with blood.*]

CARBON: We're losing ground! I've been wounded twice!

CYRANO: [*shouting to the CADETS*] Gascons! Never turn your backs! [*to CARBON, whom he is holding up*] Have no fear! I have two deaths to avenge: my friend Christian's and my own happiness! [*They come downstage, CYRANO brandishing the lance with ROXANE's handkerchief attached to it.*] Fly proudly, little lace flag embroidered with her name! [*He sticks it in the ground and shouts to the CADETS.*] Fall on them, Gascons! Crush them! [*to the FIFER*] Play, fifer!

[*The* FIFER *plays. The wounded try to rise. Some* CADETS, *falling one over the other down the slope, group themselves around* CYRANO *and the little flag. The carriage is crowded with men inside and outside. Surrounded by muskets, the carriage is protected like a fortress.*]

A CADET: [*appearing on the crest, beaten backward, but still fighting*] They're climbing up the embankment!
CYRANO: Let us salute them! [*The embankment is instantly covered by a formidable row of enemies. Imperialist flags are raised.*] Fire!

[*The* CADETS *fire.*]

A CRY FROM THE ENEMY'S RANKS: Fire!

[*There is a deadly volley of fire from the enemy. The* CADETS *fall on all sides.*]

A SPANISH OFFICER: [*taking off his hat*] Who are these men who are not afraid of death?
CYRANO: [*reciting, erect, amid a storm of bullets*] The bold cadets of Gascony, of Carbon de Castel-Jaloux! Brawling and swaggering boastfully— [*he rushes forward, followed by a few survivors*] The bold cadets...

[*His voice is drowned in the battle.*]

Curtain.

ACT V

It is fifteen years later, in 1655, at the park of the Sisters of the Holy Cross in Paris. The park is filled with magnificent trees. On the left is the house, containing broad steps onto which open several doors. An enormous plane tree is in the middle of the stage, standing alone. On the right, among big boxwood trees, is a semicircular stone bench.

The whole background of the stage is crossed by an alley of chestnut tress leading on the right-hand side to the door of a chapel seen through the branches. Through the double row of trees of this alley are seen lawns, other alleys, clusters of trees, the winding of the park, and the sky.

The chapel opens by a little side door onto a colonnade which is wreathed with autumn leaves, and is lost to view a little farther on in the right-hand foreground behind the boxwood.

It is autumn. All the foliage is red against the fresh green of the lawns. The green boxwood and yews stand out darkly. Under each tree is a patch of yellow leaves. The stage is strewn with dead leaves, which rustle under foot in the alleys, and partially cover the steps and benches.

Between the bench on the right-hand side and the tree, a large embroidery frame is set up, in front of which is a little chair. There are baskets full of skeins and balls of wool. A tapestry has been started in the frame.

At the rising of the curtain, NUNS *are walking to and fro in the park. Some are seated on the bench around an older nun. The leaves are falling.*

Scene i

MOTHER MARGUERITE, SISTER MARTHA, SISTER CLAIRE, *and other* SISTERS.

SISTER MARTHA: [*to* MOTHER MARGUERITE] Sister Claire has looked in the mirror not just once but *twice* today to see how her head-dress looks on her!

MOTHER MARGUERITE: [*to* SISTER CLAIRE] That's not good.

SISTER CLAIRE: But I saw Sister Martha steal a plum out of the tart!

MOTHER MARGUERITE: [*to* SISTER MARTHA] That was a bad deed, my sister.

SISTER CLAIRE: Just a little glance!

SISTER MARTHA: And just a little plum!

MOTHER MARGUERITE: I'll tell this to Monsieur Cyrano.

SISTER CLAIRE: Oh, please don't! He'll make fun of us!

SISTER MARTHA: He'll say that we nuns are vain!

SISTER CLAIRE: And greedy!

MOTHER MARGUERITE: [*smiling*] Yes, and kind!

SISTER CLAIRE: Is it not true, Mother Marguerite, that he has come to the convent every Saturday for ten years?

MOTHER MARGUERITE: Yes, and even longer than that. Ever since the day his cousin was brought here, wearing her widow's veil among our white habits and looking like a blackbird among a flock of white doves. That was fourteen years ago now.

SISTER MARTHA: He's the only one who can distract her from the terrible grief she still feels every day.

ALL THE SISTERS: He's so funny!—It's cheerful when he comes!—He teases us!—We like him so much!—He enjoys our pastries!

SISTER MARTHA: But he is not a faithful Catholic!

SISTER CLAIRE: We will convert him!

THE SISTERS: Yes! Yes!

MOTHER MARGUERITE: I forbid you to attempt that, my daughters. He might grow tired of it and come here less often.

SISTER MARTHA: But God—

MOTHER MARGUERITE: Do not fear! God knows him well!

SISTER MARTHA: But, every Saturday, when he arrives, he tells me, "Sister, I ate meat on Friday!"

MOTHER MARGUERITE: Oh, is that what he says? Well, the last time he came, he hadn't eaten for two whole days!

SISTER MARTHA: Mother!

MOTHER MARGUERITE: He's poor.

SISTER MARTHA: Who told you that, dear Mother?

MOTHER MARGUERITE: Monsieur Le Bret.

SISTER MARTHA: No one helps him?

MOTHER MARGUERITE: He won't permit anyone to help him. [*In an alley at the back* ROXANE *appears, dressed in black, with a widow's coif and veil.* DE GUICHE, *imposing-looking and visibly aged, walks by her side. They saunter slowly.* MOTHER MARGUERITE *rises.*] It's time we go in. Madame Madeleine walks in the garden with a visitor.

SISTER MARTHA: [*to* SISTER CLAIRE, *in a low voice*] It's the Marshal of Grammont, isn't it?

SISTER CLAIRE: [*looking at him*] Yes, I think so.

SISTER MARTHA: It's been many months since he came to see her.

THE SISTERS: He's so busy! What with the Court, the Army—

SISTER CLAIRE: His worldly concerns!

[*They go out.* DE GUICHE *and* ROXANE *come forward in silence, and stop close to the embroidery frame.*]

Scene ii

ROXANE *and the* DUKE OF GRAMMONT, *formerly* COUNT DE GUICHE. *Then* LE BRET *and* RAGUENEAU.

DUKE: And you remain here, still beautiful, still in mourning?

ROXANE: Still in mourning.

DUKE: Still faithful?

ROXANE: Still faithful.

DUKE: [*after a pause*] Do you forgive me?

ROXANE: Yes, since I've come here.

[*There is another pause.*]

DUKE: Was he really all that you say he was?

ROXANE: Yes. But he showed his true self only to those who knew him well.

DUKE: I see. Perhaps I did not know him well at all. And his last letter is always next to your heart?

ROXANE: It hangs right here on this ribbon around my neck, like a holy relic.

DUKE: And, even though he is dead, you love him still?

ROXANE: At times, it feels like he's not really dead. Our hearts still speak, as if his love is still alive, and wraps itself around me!

DUKE: [*after another pause*] Does Cyrano come to see you?

ROXANE: Oh, yes! My dear old friend never fails to come! We call him my
    "Gazette" because he brings me the news every week. His chair waits
    beneath this tree, when the weather is nice. I sit and embroider while
    I wait for him. When the clock strikes the hour of his arrival, I don't
    even turn to look, because I know that before the last stroke is heard,
    I'll hear his cane tapping down the steps. He seats himself and gently
    mocks my tapestry that's forever unfinished. He tells me all the gossip
    of the week...[LE BRET *appears on the steps.*] Why, here's Le Bret! [LE
    BRET *descends.*] How goes it with our friend?

LE BRET: Very badly!

DUKE: How?

ROXANE: [*to the* DUKE] He's exaggerating!

LE BRET: Everything I predicted is happening! Cyrano is living in poverty
    and isolating himself from the world! Everything he writes makes him
    another new enemy! He attacks false saints, false soldiers, false noble-
    men, thieving authors—everyone!

ROXANE: Ah! But his sword still holds them all in check. No one gets the
    better of him.

DUKE: [*shaking his head*] Time will tell!

LE BRET: Oh, I fear for him! But it's not the attack of men that I fear. Solitude,
    hunger, cold December days, the lonely wolf-like way he steals into his
    dreary room—these are the assassins that will come for him! Each day
    he tightens his belt one more hole. His poor nose is tinted like old ivory.
    He has only one shabby serge suit left!

DUKE: Yes, it's true, fortune hasn't smiled upon him. But he is not to
    be pitied!

LE BRET: [*with a bitter smile*] My Lord—

DUKE: Don't pity him! He has lived honestly, according to his own vows. He
    is free in his thoughts and free in his actions!

LE BRET: [*in the same tone*] My Lord, you—

DUKE: [*haughtily*] True! I have everything and he has nothing! Yet I'd
    be proud to shake his hand! [*bowing to* ROXANE] Now I must say my
    good-bye.

ROXANE: I'll walk you out.

[*The* DUKE *bows to* LE BRET *and goes with* ROXANE *toward the steps.*]

DUKE: [*pausing, while she goes up*] It's true. I do envy him sometimes. When
    a man's life is full of success, even though he hasn't acted wrongly, he
    still feels a thousand self-disgusts. It's not necessarily remorse he feels,
    but a dim, vague uneasiness. And, as he mounts the steps of worldly
    fame, he sometimes hears the sounds of dead illusions and vain regrets
    whispering and rustling among the folds of his fur-lined cloak, just as

your mourning robe sweeps the dying autumn leaves in its train as you mount the terrace steps.

ROXANE: [*ironically*] My, you're in a thoughtful mood!

DUKE: I am. [*suddenly, as he is going out*] Monsieur Le Bret! [*to* ROXANE] Will you excuse me for a moment while I have a word with him? [*He goes to* LE BRET *and speaks in a low voice.*] It's true that no one dares to attack your friend, but many do hate him. Yesterday, during a card game at court, I heard someone say, "That Cyrano may die by accident someday soon!" Tell him to be prudent and stay indoors!

LE BRET: [*raising his arms to heaven*] Prudent! Him? He's coming here today. I'll warn him, but—

ROXANE: [*who has stayed on the steps, to a* SISTER *who comes toward her*] What is it?

SISTER: Ragueneau would like to see you, Madame.

ROXANE: Let him in. [*to the* DUKE *and* LE BRET] He comes to tell me his troubles. Ever since he became an author, he's had to take jobs as a singer...

LE BRET: A bathhouse attendant...

ROXANE: An actor...

LE BRET: A beadle...

ROXANE: Wig-maker...

LE BRET: Lute-teacher...

ROXANE: I wonder what he'll be today.

RAGUENEAU: [*entering hurriedly*] Ah! Madame! [*He sees* LE BRET.] Ah! And you, Sir!

ROXANE: [*smiling*] Tell Le Bret all your troubles. I shall return shortly.

RAGUENEAU: But, Madame...

[ROXANE *goes out with the* DUKE. RAGUENEAU *goes toward* LE BRET.]

Scene iii

LE BRET, RAGUENEAU.

RAGUENEAU: I'm glad you're here! It's best that she not know! I was going to Cyrano's house just now. I was but a few steps from the house, when I saw him go out. I hurried after him. I saw him turn the corner, and suddenly, from out of a window just above him—I cannot say whether it was by accident or not—a lackey dropped a large piece of wood!

LE BRET: Cowards! Oh, Cyrano!

RAGUENEAU: I ran to him, and I saw—

LE BRET: Oh, how horrible!

RAGUENEAU: I saw our dear poet, our friend, lying on the ground with a
    large wound in his head!
LE BRET: Is he dead?
RAGUENEAU: No. I carried him to his room. Oh, what a terrible thing to see!
    That dreary little garret!
LE BRET: Is he suffering?
RAGUENEAU: No, he's unconscious.
LE BRET: Have you called a doctor?
RAGUENEAU: I found a kind doctor, and he came.
LE BRET: My poor Cyrano! We must not tell this to Roxane all at once.
    What did the doctor say?
RAGUENEAU: I don't really know! He spoke of fever, and something about
    the brain! Oh, if you could see him—his head all bound up! But let's
    hurry! There's no one by his bed, and if he tries to get up, he might
    very well die!
LE BRET: [dragging him toward the right] Come! Through the chapel! It's
    the quickest way!
ROXANE: [appearing on the steps, and seeing LE BRET go away by the col-
    onnade leading to the chapel door] Monsieur Le Bret! [LE BRET and
    RAGUENEAU disappear without answering] I call him, and he doesn't stop!
    Ragueneau's troubles must be really bad this time!

[She descends the steps.]

Scene iv

ROXANE alone. Two SISTERS, for a moment.

ROXANE: Ah! What beauty the autumn brings!† My sorrow has eased. April's
    joy sharpened it, but now September's calm comforts it. [She seats her-
    self at the embroidery frame. Two SISTERS come out of the house and set a
    large armchair under the tree.] Here is the famous armchair for my dear
    faithful friend!
SISTER MARTHA: It's the best one in the parlor!
ROXANE: Thank you, sister. [The SISTERS go.] He'll be here any moment now.
    [She seats herself. A clock strikes.] The hour strikes. I'll begin my embroi-
    dery. [after a moment] The last stroke of the hour! How strange for him
    to be late! Perhaps the sister at the door is—Where's my thimble?—is
    preaching to him. Yes, that must be it! Surely he'll come soon! Ah, a
    dead leaf. [She brushes off the leaf from her work.] Nothing could—My
    scissors? Oh yes, here in my bag—could prevent him from coming.
A SISTER: [coming to the steps] Monsieur de Bergerac.

Scene v

ROXANE, CYRANO *and, for a moment,* SISTER MARTHA.

ROXANE: [*without turning around*] What was I saying? [*She embroiders.* CYRANO, *very pale, his hat pulled down over his eyes, appears. The* SISTER *who had announced him retires. He descends the steps slowly, with a visible difficulty in holding himself upright, bearing heavily on his cane.* ROXANE *still works at her tapestry.*] The colors have faded. How can I make them match now? [*to* CYRANO, *with playful reproach*] Late for the first time in fourteen years!

CYRANO: [*He has succeeded in reaching the chair, and has seated himself, and speaks in a lively voice which is in great contrast to his pale face.*] Yes! It's scandalous! I was so angry! I was detained…

ROXANE: By?

CYRANO: By a bold, unwelcome visitor.

ROXANE: [*absently, working*] Some creditor?

CYRANO: Yes, cousin. The last creditor who has a debt to claim from me.

ROXANE: And have you paid it?

CYRANO: No, not yet! I put it off. I said, "Have mercy! This is Saturday, the day I have a standing meeting that nothing should prevent. Come back in an hour!"

ROXANE: [*carelessly*] Oh, well, a creditor can always wait! I shall not let you go before twilight falls!

CYRANO: I may have to leave you before it falls.

[*He shuts his eyes, and all is silent for a moment.* SISTER MARTHA *crosses the park from the chapel to the flight of steps.* ROXANE, *seeing her, signs for her to approach.*]

ROXANE: [*to* CYRANO] Aren't you going to tease Sister Martha today?

CYRANO: [*quickly opening his eyes*] Of course! [*in a comically loud voice*] Sister! Come here! [*The* SISTER *glides up to him.*] Such lovely eyes! Why do you always keep them cast down to the ground?

SISTER MARTHA: [*who makes a movement of astonishment upon seeing his face*] Oh!

CYRANO: [*in a whisper, pointing to* ROXANE] Hush! It's nothing! [*loudly, in a blustering voice*] I ate meat yesterday!

SISTER MARTHA: [*aside*] He must be pale from hunger! [*to* CYRANO, *in a whisper*] Come into the refectory soon and I'll make you a bowl of soup! Will you come?

CYRANO: Yes, yes!

SISTER MARTHA: Ah! You're more reasonable today than usual!

ROXANE: [*who hears them whispering*] Is the sister trying to convert you?

SISTER MARTHA: No, not I!

CYRANO: It's true! You with your holy words! You used to preach to me all the time, but not anymore! I'm astonished! [*with mock fury*] Well, I can astonish you too! Listen here! I permit you... [*He pretends to be seeking for something to tease her with, and to have found it.*] I've got it! I permit you to pray for me tonight at chapel!

ROXANE: Oh!

CYRANO: [*laughing*] Good Sister Martha is struck speechless!

SISTER MARTHA: [*gently*] I've never waited for your permission.

[*She goes out.*]

CYRANO: [*turning to* ROXANE, *who is still bending over her work*] That tapestry! Will I ever see the end of that eternal thing?

ROXANE: I've been waiting for you to make fun of it!

[*A light breeze causes the leaves to fall.*]

CYRANO: The autumn leaves!

ROXANE: [*lifting her head, and looking down the distant alley*] Golden brown and red, like a painting by Titian.[†] See how they fall!

CYRANO: Ah, see how bravely they fall. Still lovely, even on their last short journey to the ground, where they'll rot within the clay. They hide the horror of that end by floating down so carelessly and gracefully!

ROXANE: You sound melancholy!

CYRANO: [*collecting himself*] No, no, Roxane!

ROXANE: Then let the dead leaves fall as they will. Chat with me. Haven't you any news to tell, my Court Gazette?

CYRANO: I'll begin right now.

ROXANE: Good!

CYRANO: [*growing whiter and whiter, struggling against pain*] On Saturday, the nineteenth, after having eaten several helpings of pear jelly, the King felt feverish. The court physician convicted the illness of high treason and executed it, and now the royal pulse beats at a normal pace once again. At the Queen's ball on Sunday, seven hundred wax candles were burned. Our troops, they say, have chased away John of Austria.[†] Four witches were hanged. The little dog of Madame d'Athis had an enema—

ROXANE: That's enough, Monsieur de Bergerac!

CYRANO: On Monday, not much happened. Lygdamire took a new lover.

ROXANE: Oh!

CYRANO: [*whose face changes more and more*] On Tuesday, the Court went off to Fontainebleau.† On Wednesday, Madame Montglat said "No" to Count de Fiesque. On Thursday, Olympe Mancini† became the Queen of France—well, almost! On Friday, Madame Montglat said "Yes" to Count de Fiesque. And today, Saturday the twenty-sixth...

[*He closes his eyes. His head falls forward. There is silence.*]

ROXANE: [*surprised at his voice ceasing, turns around, looks at him, and rises, terrified*] He's fainted! [*She runs toward him, crying.*] Cyrano!
CYRANO: [*opening his eyes, in a vague voice*] What's this? [*He sees* ROXANE *bending over him and hastily presses his hat on his head and shrinks back in his chair.*] It's nothing! I swear! Let me be!
ROXANE: But—
CYRANO: It's just that old wound from Arras acting up. It hurts sometimes.
ROXANE: Dear friend!
CYRANO: 'Tis nothing. It will pass soon. [*He smiles with an effort.*] See! It has passed already!
ROXANE: Each of us has his own wound. I have mine, too. It still hasn't healed up, my old wound! [*She puts her hand on her breast.*] 'Tis here, beneath this letter brown with age, all stained with tears and blood.

[*Twilight begins to fall.*]

CYRANO: His letter! You promised that one day you would let me read it.
ROXANE: Do you really want to read it?
CYRANO: Yes, I do. In fact, I'd like to read it right now.
ROXANE: [*removing the little bag which hangs from her neck*] Here it is!
CYRANO: [*taking it*] Do I have your permission to open it?
ROXANE: Yes, open it and read!

[*She goes back to her tapestry frame, folds it up, and sorts her wools.*]

CYRANO: [*reading*] Goodbye, Roxane! I soon must die! My soul is heavy with love untold. No more shall my eyes feast on your smallest gestures. I think of the way you touch your cheek, softly, with your finger, as you speak! I know that gesture so well! My heart cries out, and I cry, "Farewell!"
ROXANE: How well you read that letter! It's as if...
CYRANO: [*continuing to read*] My life, my love, my jewel, my sweet! My heart has been yours in every beat!

[*The shades of evening fall imperceptibly.*]

ROXANE: You read in such a voice! A voice I've heard somewhere before!

[*She comes nearer very softly, without his perceiving it, passes behind his chair, and, noiselessly leaning over him, looks at the letter. The darkness deepens.*]

CYRANO: My heart has never left you. In this world and in the next, I am
     the one who loves you—
ROXANE: [*putting her hand on his shoulder*] How can you read? It's too dark
     to see! [*He starts, turns, sees her close to him. Suddenly alarmed, he holds
     his head down. Then in the dusk, which has now completely enfolded them,
     she speaks, very slowly, with clasped hands.*] And, for fourteen years now,
     he has played the part of the kind old friend who comes to laugh and
     chat.
CYRANO: Roxane!
ROXANE: It was you!
CYRANO: No, Roxane, no!
ROXANE: I should have guessed it each time you said my name!
CYRANO: No, it was not I!
ROXANE: It was you!
CYRANO: I swear!
ROXANE: I see through the whole generous lie! The letters—you!
CYRANO: No!
ROXANE: The sweet, mad love-words! All yours!
CYRANO: No!
ROXANE: That voice that thrilled me in the night! You!
CYRANO: I swear you're mistaken.
ROXANE: The soul—it was your soul!
CYRANO: I loved you not!
ROXANE: You *did* love me!
CYRANO: No! It was he!
ROXANE: You loved me!
CYRANO: [*in a weakening voice*] No!
ROXANE: You're faltering now. You're denying it less strongly.
CYRANO: No, my sweet love, I never loved you!
ROXANE: Ah! So many long-dead things are being reborn now! Why did you
     keep your silence all these fourteen years when the tears on this letter,
     which he never wrote, are your tears?
CYRANO: [*holding out the letter to her*] The blood is his.
ROXANE: Why, then, have you broken your noble silence today?
CYRANO: Why?...

[LE BRET *and* RAGUENEAU *enter running.*]

Scene vi

The same, with LE BRET *and* RAGUENEAU.

LE BRET: What madness! He's here! I knew it!

CYRANO: [*smiling and sitting up*] Of course I am! What is it?

LE BRET: Madame, he has brought his death by coming here.

ROXANE: Oh, God! That moment just now, when you fainted—!

CYRANO: Ah, yes! The moment that so rudely interrupted the "Gazette." As I was saying, on Saturday, the twenty-sixth, at dinner-time, Monsieur de Bergerac was murdered.

[*He takes off his hat. They all see that his head is bandaged.*]

ROXANE: What is he talking about? Cyrano! Those bandages! What's happened? How? Who?

CYRANO: To be struck down by a sword in the heart, from a worthy opponent's hand! That's what I had dreamed of! Oh, how Fate mocks me! I, of all men, killed in an ambush! Struck from behind, and by a lackey's hand! 'Tis very fitting. I've failed in everything, even in death.

RAGUENEAU: Oh, Sir!

CYRANO: [*holding out his hand to him*] Ragueneau, don't weep so bitterly! What are you doing for money now, old comrade?

RAGUENEAU: [*amid his tears*] I snuff out the lights in the theater. I work for Molière.†

CYRANO: Molière!

RAGUENEAU: Yes, but I'm quitting tomorrow. I cannot bear it! Yesterday, they played *Scapin*,† and they used a scene stolen from you!†

LE BRET: The whole scene!

RAGUENEAU: Yes, the famous one: "What the devil is he doing?"

LE BRET: Molière stole that from you!

CYRANO: Hush! I'm glad he took it. Tell me, how was the scene?

RAGUENEAU: [*sobbing*] Oh! It was wonderful! The audience laughed and laughed!

CYRANO: It's been my life's role to prompt others to greatness and to be forgotten myself. [*to* ROXANE] Do you remember that night, when Christian spoke to you from under your balcony? Well, there was the allegory of my whole life: I stand in the shadows, at the foot of the ladder, while others lightly climb their way up to Love and Fame! Here, on the threshold of death, I see the justice of it—Molière has genius and Christian had beauty! [*The chapel-bell chimes. The nuns are seen passing down the alley at the back, to say their prayers.*] Let them go pray. Their bell is ringing!

ROXANE: [*rising and calling*] Sister! Sister!

CYRANO: [*holding her fast*] Don't go after them! If you leave me, I'll be gone for good when you come back. [*The nuns have all entered the chapel. The organ sounds.*] Ah! I was in need of some music, and here it is!

ROXANE: Please live! I love you!

CYRANO: In fairy tales, when the lady says "I love you" to the beast, his ugliness disappears. But this is no fairy tale. I remain the same, even after you speak the magic words.

ROXANE: I am the source of your life's unhappiness! I!

CYRANO: No. You have blessed my life! Never in my life had I been loved by a woman. Even my mother could not see past my ugliness. I had no sister and, when grown a man, I feared all women would mock me. But I have had your gracious friendship. Because of you, a woman's charm has finally passed across my path.

LE BRET: [*pointing to the moon, which is seen between the trees*] Your other lady-love has come.

CYRANO: [*smiling*] I see.

ROXANE: I loved one man, and now I've lost him twice!

CYRANO: Tonight, Le Bret, I shall reach the moon, without the aid of any projectile!

LE BRET: What are you saying?

CYRANO: I tell you, it's there that I'll have my Paradise. There I shall find at last the exiled souls that I love—Galileo,[†] Socrates[†]...

LE BRET: [*rebelliously*] No, no! This is too unjust! So great a poet! So great a heart! To die like this?

CYRANO: Listen to Le Bret, always scolding!

LE BRET: [*weeping*] Dear friend...

CYRANO: [*starting up, his eyes wild*] The bold cadets of Gascony!...The elemental mass!...Ah, yes!...There's the thing...

LE BRET: Still speaking science, even in his delirium.

CYRANO: Copernicus[†] said...

ROXANE: Oh!

CYRANO: "But what the devil was he doing there? What the devil was he doing there, on that galley?" [*He declaims.*] Philosopher, physician, poet, brawler, musician; famed for his lunar expedition and for duels and battles no less; and lover too, to his own distress! Here lies Hercule Savinien de Cyrano de Bergerac, who was everything yet was nothing. I beg your pardon, but I cannot stay. See, the moon's rays come to call me up! [*He has fallen back in his chair. The sobs of* ROXANE *call him back to reality. He looks for a long moment at her and touches her veil.*] I would not ask you to mourn that good, brave Christian less faithfully. I would only ask that when my body is cold and in the ground, that you wear your mourning clothes for two, and mourn me for a while, as you mourn him.

ROXANE: I swear I will!

CYRANO: [*shivering violently, then suddenly rising*] No! Not seated! [*They all spring toward him.*] Let no one hold me up! [*He props himself up against the tree.*] Only this tree! [*There is silence.*] It comes. Even now my feet have turned to stone. My hands are heavy like lead. [*He stands erect.*] But since Death comes, I'll meet him standing. [*He draws his sword.*] And with sword in hand!

LE BRET: Cyrano!

ROXANE: [*half fainting*] Cyrano!

[*Everyone shrinks back in terror.*]

CYRANO: I see him! He, the noseless one, dares to mock my nose! How insolent! [*He raises his sword.*] You say it's useless. That I know. But who fights believing that every battle will be a success? I fought for lost causes and fruitless quests! You there! I see you! Thousands of you! All enemies of mine, I know you now! Ah! There's Falsehood! [*He strikes the air with his sword.*] And Compromise! Prejudice! Treachery! [*He strikes.*] Will I surrender? Strike an agreement? Never! And there you are, Folly! I know you'll be the one to take me down, at last. Yet I'll fall fighting, fighting still! [*He makes passes in the air, and stops, breathless.*] You've stripped me of the laurel and the rose! Of glory and love! Take it all! But there is still one thing I hold against you, and when I enter God's house tonight, I shall wave one thing in salutation, across heaven's blue threshold. For there is one thing I have left, void of smear or stain, and I take it with me despite you. [*He springs forward, his sword raised. It falls from his hand. He staggers and falls back into the arms of* LE BRET *and* RAGUENEAU.]

ROXANE: [*bending and kissing his forehead*] And that is—?

CYRANO: [*opening his eyes, recognizing her, and smiling*] My white plume.†

Curtain.

Glossary

Dedication

Coquelin – Benoît-Constant Coquelin (1841 – 1909) was Edmond Rostand's
favorite actor and played the part of Cyrano de Bergerac when the play
first opened in 1897. It is said that Rostand wrote Cyrano de Bergerac
specifically for Coquelin so that he could play the title role.

Dramatis Personae

Cyrano de Bergerac – The character of Cyrano de Bergerac is based on a real
person, Savinien Cyrano de Bergerac (1619 – 1655), who was a novelist,
playwright, and soldier living during the time in which the play is set.
While Edmond Rostand based his character on the real Cyrano, the events
and the storyline of the play are mainly fictional, as is Cyrano's extremely
large nose.

Act I, Scene i

Hotel de Bourgogne – [*French*] Hotel Burgundy; a theater built on the site
where the Dukes of Burgundy had lived during the 14th and 15th cen-
turies. The fact that the opening scene occurs in a theater highlights the
importance of the theater in 17th century France. Notice how nearly all
members of society are represented at the theater—from pickpockets to
aristocrats.

sols – coins used in France during the Middle Ages; twenty sols equaled one
Tournoise pound—the basic form of currency during that period.

"I'm a soldier in the King's Cavalry!" – Any soldier, musketeer, or royal
official was allowed free admission into the theater. Actors were
opposed to this practice because their pay was based on ticket sales.
The playwright Molière eventually succeeded in getting Louis XIV to
put an end to the practice.

Burgundy – a variety of wine grown in the Burgundy region of France

Rotrou – Jean de Rotrou (1609 – 1650) was a French playwright who
worked under the patronage of Cardinal Richelieu during the time in
which the play is set.

Corneille – Pierre Corneille (1606 – 1684), a French playwright considered to
have mastered the art of classical tragedy; he is best known for his tragedy
"Le Cid" (1637).

Balthazar Baro – (1600 – 1650), a French playwright and novelist

the 'Cid' – a reference to a 1637 play by Pierre Corneille (see note: *Corneille*
above) about El Cid (1043 – 1099), a legendary Spanish military leader
during the 11th century, who later became the subject of an epic poem
and many plays

Montfleury; "**Bellerose, L'Epy, La Beaupre, Jodelet!**" – actual French actors from the time in which the play is set

Act I, Scene ii

Touraine – a region in west central France

"**Tomorrow I join the Guards, in the Cadets.**" – A cadet in 17th century France was a nobleman who enlisted as a soldier in order to gain experience for the future goal of becoming an officer. During the time of *Cyrano*, France was involved in the Thirty Years' War (1618 – 1648), which was mainly a war over trade routes. The war pitted France and its allies against the Holy Roman Empire.

Rouen – a city in northern France located on the Seine River

the Academy – the French Academy; a society of intellectuals and writers founded in 1635 and still in existence today. Rostand himself was inducted into the French Academy in 1901.

Jacques Callot – (1592 – 1635), a French artist, famous for his caricatures

Gascony – a region in southwest France

Armand de Richelieu – Cardinal Richelieu (1585 – 1642) was the Prime Minister of France and one of the major religious leaders during the reign of King Louis XIII. He was also a supporter of the arts and founded the French Academy.

Act I, Scene iii

'**Sick Spaniard**' – 'Sick Spaniard' is de Guiche's derogatory reference to the Spanish. Both countries, France and Spain, were fighting for control over Flanders, a region in the Netherlands.

Act I, Scene iv

Thalia – In Greek mythology, Thalia was the muse of comedy and pastoral poetry.

"**Samson…jawbone**" – an allusion to the biblical story of Samson; in the Old Testament, Samson killed an army of Philistines with the jawbone of a donkey.

Thespis – a Greek poet who lived during the sixth century BC; Thespis is commonly credited as the inventor of the Greek tragedy. The word *thespian*, which means "actor," derives from *Thespis*.

Aristophanes' hippocampelephantocamelos – Aristophanes was a Greek playwright during the fourth century BC who wrote comedies and satires. The *hippocampelephantocamelos* is an imaginary beast created by Aristophanes. It has the characteristics of a seahorse, an elephant, and a camel.

Triton – In ancient Greek mythology, Triton was the messenger of the sea.

He carried a conch shell, which he used as a trumpet. Cyrano is likening his own nose to Triton's enormous and loud conch shell.

"...**Pyramus 'Behold...the traitor!'**" – In ancient Roman mythology, Pyramus, who was in love with Thisbe, committed suicide because he mistakenly thought that Thisbe had been killed. The reference is to a 17th century play by Théophile de Viau called *Les Amours tragiques de Pyrame et Thisbé*. The line that Cyrano parodies is the following: "Here is the dagger that basely sullied itself with its master's blood. It is red with shame, the traitor!"

Phoebus – one of the names, along with *Apollo*, for the ancient Greek god of the sun

"...**at the end of the refrain...I strike!**" – Note how Cyrano literally fights his opponent with words as well as with a sword. Cyrano's prowess as a swordsman and a poet testifies to both his physical and intellectual skills.

D'Artagnan – Charles de Batz-Castelmore d'Artagnan (c.1611 – 1673) was a heroic French soldier under King Louis XIV. Alexandre Dumas (1802 – 1870) immortalized d'Artagnan in his 1844 novel *The Three Musketeers*. *Cyrano de Bergerac* both parodies and pays tribute to this book. Look for more references to *The Three Musketeers* throughout the play.

Sic transit – [*Latin*] a shortening of the phrase *sic transit gloria mundi*, which translates to "thus passes the glory of the world"; with this phrase, Bellerose uses sarcasm to make fun of Montfleury.

Act I, Scene v

Cupid – the Roman god of love

Venus – the Roman goddess of love

Diana – the Roman goddess of the hunt

"...**Caesar...Cleopatra?**" – Julius Caesar (100 BC – 44 BC) ruled the Roman Empire from 59 BC until his death. Cleopatra (69 BC – 30 BC) was the Queen of Egypt. The two were lovers and had a son together.

"...**Tito...Berenice?**" – Tito refers to Roman Emperor Titus (39 AD – 81 AD); Berenice was a Jewish princess born around 28 AD. They were in love, although Romans generally opposed their marriage. Cyrano's insecurity regarding his nose is apparent when he compares himself to this couple. He believes himself unable to attain love because of his physical appearance.

Act I, Scene vi

–

Act I, Scene vii

Scipio – Publius Cornelius Scipio Africanus (c.236 BC – 183 BC) was a Roman general who conquered North Africa during the second Punic War.

Seine – a river in northern France flowing through Paris and other major cities

Act II, Scene i

Malherbe – François de Malherbe (1555 – 1628) was a French poet who proposed strict and rigid rules for poetry.

"...Bacchantes...Orpheus!" – In ancient Roman mythology, the Bacchantes were female followers of Bacchus, the god of wine. Seeing Orpheus one day, they set upon him in a frenzy of lust, tearing him to pieces and killing him.

Act II, Scene ii

"Ulysses...Penelope..." – Ulysses (also called Odysseus) was the hero of Homer's epic poem the *Odyssey*, written in the eighth century BC. The line refers specifically to the moment when Odysseus must leave his wife, Penelope, in order to fight in the Trojan War.

Act II, Scene iii

—

Act II, Scene iv

Apollo – In ancient Greek mythology, Apollo was the god of the sun (see note: *Phoebus* in Act I, Scene iv).

Act II, Scene v

Monsieur Benserade – a reference to the French poet and playwright Isaac de Benserade (1613 – 1691)

Saint Amant – a reference to the French poet Antoine Girard de Saint-Amant (1594 – 1661)

Chapelain – a reference to another French poet, Jean Chapelain (1595 – 1674); both Chapelain and Saint-Amant were original members of the French Academy.

Act II, Scene vi

"one of d'Urfe's heroes" – a reference to the works of the French novelist Honoré d'Urfé (1568 – 1625); the heroes of d'Urfé's stories were considered perfect models of knights.

Act II, Scene vii

"Sandious!" – a Gascon exclamation of distress or surprise

Marais – a neighborhood in Paris; up until the 18th century, the Marais was considered the most fashionable and aristocratic neighborhood in Paris.

"Théophraste Renaudot...the 'Gazette'" – In 1631, Théophraste Renaudot (1586 – 1653) founded *La Gazette*, the first French newspaper.

Agrippine – a reference to *La Mort d'Agrippine*, a play written by the real Cyrano de Bergerac

Don Quixote – a novel written by Miguel de Cervantes (1547 – 1616) in 1605; the reference is to the part of the story in which the foolish, idealistic hero, Don Quixote, imagines that windmills are giants and tries to fight them.

Act II, Scene viii

"I'll pay no tribute to Caesar" – Cyrano means that he will pay nothing to anyone in power because all the achievement would be his own; this references the tributes paid to Julius Caesar during his reign as emperor.

"Whether I rise very high or not...I climb alone!" – This line comes at the end of Cyrano's long and poignant speech about refusing to seek a patron. During the time in which the play is set, many artists and poets sought patronage from wealthy aristocrats to live well and practice their craft. In some ways, these artists would end up compromising their ideals in order to please their patrons. Clearly, Cyrano hates the idea of patronage. An important aspect of his character is his refusal of any kind of aid and his goal to remain free at all costs. The fictional Cyrano hates patronage, as did the real Cyrano, although the latter did end up, out of necessity, accepting the patronage of the Duke of Arpajon.

Act II, Scene ix

"MORDIOUS!" – a Gascon curse word, translated loosely as "like death"

Act II, Scene x

"Let my words...together!" – This line prepares the reader for the main action that occurs throughout the rest of the play. Cyrano and Christian will conspire together to win Roxane, using Cyrano's wit and Christian's beauty. Together they will create one perfect romantic hero. This plan, however, is full of deception and leads to unintended consequences.

Act II, Scene xi

—

Act III, Scene i
Mars – In Roman mythology, Mars was the god of war.

"She's receiving…'The Tender Passion'" – In France during the 17th century, literary works were often read and discussed at a noblewoman's house. These gatherings were referred to as salons and were attended by writers, philosophers, and intellectuals. Madeleine Robineau, the woman upon whom Roxane's character is based, frequently attended and hosted salons.

"demi-semi-quaver" – a musical term for a particular note and its duration; the literal meaning is one thirty-second of a whole note.

Gassendi – Pierre Gassendi (1592 – 1655) was a French scientist, philosopher, and mathematician. The actual Cyrano de Bergerac is believed to have been one of his students.

Act III, Scene ii
Arras – Originally part of the Spanish Netherlands, Arras was captured by the French during the time in which the play is set and remains a French city today. The siege of Arras, which is the setting for Act IV, took place in 1640. The real Cyrano de Bergerac and the real Baron de Neuvillette both fought in the siege, and the real Baron de Neuvillette died during it.

Capuchins – Franciscan monks belonging to the Order of Friars Minor Capuchin, founded in Italy around 1525

Act III, Scenes iii – v
—

Act III, Scene vi
Hercules – a hero in ancient Greek mythology known for his strength

Act III, Scene vii
Diogenes – a Greek philosopher who lived around 300 BC; Diogenes is said to have wandered through the streets of Athens with a lantern in search of an honest man.

Act III, Scene viii
—

Act III, Scene ix
"I have suffered…queen." – a reference to Alexandre Dumas' novel *The Three Musketeers*. In the novel, Dumas fictionalizes a romance between George Villiers, Duke of Buckingham (1592 – 1628) and Queen Anne of Austria (1601 – 1666).

"**Lazarus at the feast**" – In one of the parables in the New Testament, Lazarus is a beggar at a rich man's feast. He is refused food, but is later rewarded in Heaven when the rich man must beg Lazarus for a drop of water.

Act III, Scene x
pistoles – gold coins

Act III, Scene xi
Venice – a city in northeast Italy
"**the Great Bear**" – a reference to the constellation Ursa Major
Neptune – the Roman god of the sea
"**the Scales**" – a reference to the constellation Libra, which is in the shape of a balance or weighing scales
Sirius – a reference to the brightest star in the sky
The other Bear – a reference to the constellation Ursa Minor
the Lyre –the name of a constellation
"**Some day…in a book!**" – Rostand is using a fact involving the real Cyrano de Bergerac, who wrote and published several fantastic stories describing voyages to the moon, complete with imaginative methods of space travel similar to the ones in the play.
Regiomontanus' eagle…Archytas' pigeon – Regiomontanus is the nickname of Johannes Muller (1436 – 1476); Muller was a German astronomer and mathematician who supposedly invented a mechanical eagle that could fly. Archytas (428 BC – 347 BC) was a Greek philosopher and astronomer who also supposedly built a flying artificial bird.

Act III, Scene xii
—

Act IV, Scene i
Cardinal Infante of Spain – Cardinal-Infante Ferdinand (1610 – 1641) was the Prince of Spain and the Governor of the Spanish Netherlands

Act IV, Scene ii
Achilles – the hero of Homer's epic poem *The Iliad*, written in the 8th century BC; the cadet is referring to the part of the story in which Achilles, angry with his leader Agamemnon, withdraws his troops from fighting in the Trojan War and sulks in his tent.

Act IV, Scene iii
The Iliad – an epic poem written by Homer in the 8th century BC; Cyrano

seems to be making a point by throwing this particular book at the cadet. As explained previously, the hero, Achilles, refuses to fight for the Greeks out of anger. However, he ends up returning to the war out of a need for vengeance after his friend is killed. The idea of the hero, and the question of what makes a hero, are important themes in *The Iliad*. It seems as though Cyrano wants the cadet to stop complaining and think about these things.

"The prime minister in Paris..." – a reference to Cardinal Richelieu (1585 – 1642), who was King Louis XIII's Chief Minister. King Louis's weak leadership qualities allowed Richelieu to advise the king and ultimately rule the empire. Richelieu is sometimes referred to as the first Prime Minister (see note: *Armand de Richelieu* in Act I, Scene ii).

Dordogne River – a river flowing through parts of France

Descartes – René Descartes (1596 – 1650) was a French philosopher and mathematician. Considered to be the father of modern philosophy, Descartes is most famous for concluding, "I think, therefore I am."

Act IV, Scene iv

Bapaume – a municipality of the town of Arras, France

Count of Bucquoi – a Flemish general during the Thirty Years' War

"...Henry the Fourth would never...scarf" – At the battle of Ivry in 1590, King Henry IV of France (1553 – 1610) refused to retreat, even though he was greatly outnumbered by the enemy. He is said to have told his soldiers to follow his white plume; doing so would lead them on the path to honor and glory. In the play, the white scarf is a symbol of honor, bravery, and idealism. While de Guiche throws it aside to aid himself in a maneuver, Cyrano braves the Spanish lines in order to retrieve it.

Act IV, Scenes v – vii

—

Act IV, Scene viii

Helen – According to ancient Greek mythology, Helen was the most beautiful woman in the world. Her abduction by Paris was the incident that set off the Trojan War.

"I would love you...became ugly—" – Roxane's statement illuminates an important theme of the play: the idea that inner beauty is more substantial than outer beauty, and that intelligence is more important than appearance. The statement also emphasizes the irony that is occurring during the scene. While Roxane believes that her statement will make Christian realize that she loves him for his inner worth, Christian hears the statement as proof that she does not love him for who he is at all.

Her love belongs, instead, to the person who wrote the letters. While Christian and the audience know that Cyrano wrote the letters, Roxane is unaware.

Act IV, Scene ix
—

Act IV, Scene x
"Ready your matches!" – Matches were pieces of burning cord that were used to ignite the explosives in a musket.

Act V, Scenes i – iii
—

Act V, Scene iv
"What beauty the autumn brings!" – Since autumn is symbolic of the onset of death, it is fitting that the action in Act V occurs in the autumn.

Act V, Scene v
Titian – Tiziano Vecellio (c.1488 – 1576), an Italian painter, noted for his use of vivid and rich colors
John of Austria – (1629 – 1679) a Spanish general who was defeated by the French in 1658
Fontainebleau – a town about forty miles from Paris containing a magnificent palace that served as a residence for French Royalty
Olympe Mancini – (1638 – 1708), a mistress of Louis XIV

Act V, Scene vi
Molière – Originally named Jean-Baptiste Poquelin, Molière (1622 – 1673) was a famous French playwright who owned his own theatre company and wrote plays for it; many of them were classified as sophisticated comedies.
Scapin – a 1671 farce by Molière
"...they used a scene stolen from you!" – While it is true that Molière did use the real Cyrano's lines in his play *Scapin*, Cyrano could not have known this because the play was written sixteen years after the actual Cyrano died.
Galileo – Galileo Galilei (1564 – 1642), an Italian astronomer and mathematician who was the first to look at the sky through a telescope; Galileo confirmed Copernicus's theory that the planets revolve around the sun. Because of this confirmation, Galileo was tried for heresy by the church and forced to recant his ideas.

Socrates – (469 BC – 399 BC), a Greek philosopher who spent his life searching for moral truths; as an old man, Socrates was charged with heresy and the corruption of youth. Found guilty of the charges, he was sentenced to death by the lawmakers in Athens. He performed his own execution by drinking poisonous hemlock, and since then, he has been considered a martyr for philosophy and truth seeking.

Copernicus – Nicolaus Copernicus (1473 – 1543) was a Polish astronomer and mathematician who theorized that Earth was not the center of the universe and that Earth and other planets revolved around the sun; his radical discovery is considered to be the starting point of the scientific revolution (see note: *Galileo* above).

"My white plume." – Note again the symbolic significance of the white plume, which represents honor, bravery, and idealism (see note: *"...Henry the Fourth would never...scarf"* in Act IV, Scene iv).

Vocabulary

ACT I, Scene i
burghers – middle-class citizens (bourgeois); merchants
falsetto – a high-pitched male voice
foils – fencing swords
lackeys – low-level servants
marquises – noblemen who rank one below the ranking of a duke
oblong – rectangular
pages – messenger servants
proscenium – an area of a theater between the orchestra and the curtain
troopers – soldiers on horseback; cavalrymen

ACT I, Scene ii
candelabra – a candle holder that holds several candles at once; a chandelier
   with candles
coquettish – flirtatious
duenna – a governess; chaperone
ode – a type of lyric poem usually addressed directly to a particular idea or
   object
triolet – a type of poem containing eight lines in each stanza, with the
   first line repeated as the fourth and seventh lines and the second line
   repeated as the eighth line

ACT I, Scene iii
incredulously – skeptically; in disbelief
obsequious – submissive, fawning
pastoral – pertaining to the pleasant country life; rural
persecute – to oppress or harass
viscount – a nobleman whose rank is one below that of an earl

ACT I, Scene iv
affable – pleasant, friendly
appendage – an attachment (usually referring to a part of the body)
conch – a type of large shell
envoi – a short passage at the end of a poem
farce – a comedic play containing much slapstick and a far-fetched plot
parry – to deflect; to sidestep
pedantic – excessively wordy in a pretentious way
scabbard – a case for a sword
tragedian – an actor who plays tragic characters

ACT I, Scene v
protuberance – something that projects outward; a lump or bulge
sublime – inspiring; of the highest moral worth

ACT I, Scene vi
—

ACT I, Scene vii
nebulous – hazy, vague, unclear

ACT II, Scene i
andiron – a metal support used in a fireplace
couplet – two lines of poetry usually rhyming and having the same rhythm
desecrated – defiled, violated
diminutive – small
gallery – a narrow passageway
lute – a small guitar-like musical instrument
lyre – a stringed instrument belonging to the harp family
scullions – kitchen workers

ACT II, Scenes ii – iii
—

ACT II, Scene iv
cudgels – small, heavy clubs
pikes – long spears

ACT II, Scenes v – vi
—

ACT II, Scene vii
coronets – crowns worn by members of the noble class
heraldry – the study of genealogy, coats of arms, and ranks of the noble class
intrepid – brave
pentacrostic – a set of five lines of poetry in which the same word or name is formed within all five lines

ACT II, Scene viii
madrigals – vocal arrangements meant to be sung by three voices in harmony with one another

ACT II, Scene ix
—

ACT II, Scene x
eloquence – the ability to express oneself gracefully and fluently
haphazard – random

ACT III, Scene i
livery – a uniform worn by male household servants
steward – one who manages a household or property
trite – unoriginal, commonplace

ACT III, Scene ii
syndic – an officer of a particular organization who carries out certain duties

ACT III, Scene iii
discourse – to talk; to discuss

ACT III, Scenes iv – v
—

ACT III, Scene vi
embellishments – trimmings; added extras
premeditated – planned, intentional

ACT III, Scene vii
rosary – a string of beads used for counting prayers

ACT III, Scenes viii – x
—

ACT III, Scene x
discreet – tactful, restrained
martyr – a sacrificial victim; one who suffers

ACT III, Scene xi
asterisks – star-shaped symbols used in writing
metaphorically – figuratively, symbolically
posterior – the rear
rarefied – made thin or less dense
trident – a three-pointed spear

Act IV, Scene i

besiegers – those who surround and blockade an area hoping to capture it from an enemy

embankment – a protective wall

entrenchments – ditches cut into the ground

sentinels – guards, watchmen

Act IV, Scene ii

mutiny – an open rebellion against those in charge

reveille – a signal played on the bugle or the drum in order to awaken soldiers in the morning

wadding – stuffing or padding

Act IV, Scene iii

adversary – an enemy, opponent

courtier – an aristocrat; a member of the nobility

gluttonous – greedy, voracious

hearthstones – literally, the stones that make up the area in front of a fireplace; symbolically, hearths or hearthstones represent "home"

minuet – a type of dance that originated in France during the 17th century

pastoral – idyllic, rustic

patois – a regional dialect

ravenous – extremely hungry

Act IV, Scene iv

abdicating – giving up; relinquishing

Act IV, Scene v

ceremoniously – grandly; in a royal or noble way

Act IV, Scene vi

galantine – a type of sauce for fish or chicken; a dish made with such a sauce

gallantry – chivalry, courtesy; bravery

lance – a type of spear

pantry – a food cupboard

topaz – any of several gemstones that are yellow in color

truffles – small mushrooms considered a delicacy

Act IV, Scene vii

pikemen – infantrymen who carry pikes (long spears)

recoil – the jerking-back movement that a gun or cannon makes upon firing

ACT IV, Scene viii
frivolous – thoughtless, careless

ACT IV, Scene ix
—

ACT IV, Scene x
formidable – alarming; frighteningly impressive
imperialist – of or relating to an empire
ramrods – rods used for stuffing the charge into a firearm

ACT V, Scene i
coif – a small, tight-fitting cap
colonnade – a passageway consisting of uniformly spaced columns
habits – distinctive modes of dress (robes etc.) for members of religious
   orders
skeins – loose coils of yarn

ACT V, Scene ii
beadle – one who delivers public announcements; a town crier
haughtily – proudly, arrogantly
prudent – sensible, wise
relic – an object of religious reverence and significance
serge – a type of cloth made from wool

ACT V, Scene III
garret – an attic room

ACT V, Scene iv
—

ACT V, Scene v
imperceptibly – unnoticeably, undetectably
refectory – a dining hall

ACT V, Scene vi
allegory – a story that is written symbolically to represent didactic ideals or
   abstract notions
delirium – in a state of frenzy, confusion, disorientation
exiled – banished; sent away
insolent – rude, disrespectful
projectile – an object that is propelled in some way, like a rocket or a
   bullet
salutation – a greeting